When the Calls Stop

RETIRING AS A

FIRST RESPONDER

Mynda Ohs, PhD

ISBNs: 978-0-578-39387-2 (pbk); 978-0-578-39388-9 (ebook)

Front cover photograph courtesy of Allison Hays, Retired Fire Wife
Cover and book design by Mayfly Design

Library of Congress Catalog Number: 2022905377
First Printing: 2022
Printed in the United States of America

Contents

Part Three: What to Do Now, Then, and Later

For All First Responder Families

M y son-in-law Bryce became part of a first responder family by default. A musician in Las Vegas, he married into it.
While my daughter Megan's career is in juvenile corrections,
her husband happens to have several friends who, like my husband Jeff and our son Kyle, are firefighters. Not long after my
first book, *Fully Involved: A Guide for Being in a Relationship with a
Firefighter*, was published, Bryce had an experience that shocked
and amazed me.

He was hanging out with a musician buddy who had some
firefighter friends visiting from California. What happened next
was like "Six Degrees of Kevin Bacon," because these Orange
County firefighters started talking about this book they had all
read and how much it had impacted their lives.

When Bryce asked them the name of it, he was surprised by
their response. "My mother-in-law wrote that," he told them,
and they reacted excitedly as if he had told them he was related
to a celebrity. I'm not a celebrity, of course. I'm just Dr. Mynda
Ohs, a former EMT working for a private ambulance company
who married a firefighter and paramedic. When I found myself
a stay-at-home mom whose husband lived at the fire station half
the time while I had most of my conversations with a small child
and an even smaller toddler, I headed back to school—initially
for the opportunity to socialize, never dreaming I would find my
passion in psychology.

I made the perfect choice after getting my doctorate: to specialize in helping first responders. As my husband left CDF, now Cal Fire, and started over at Long Beach City Fire Department, he focused on climbing the departmental ladder on the way to becoming a battalion chief. Meanwhile, I expanded my clinical practice to include first responder spouses, because they inhabit a world as unusual as their partners. Fire families—and, indeed, all first responder families—are not like other families. We enjoy unique blessings and benefits, but also face unique problems. Out of my personal experience, and that of my clients, came my guide for helping fire families normalize and resolve the challenges of being in a relationship that is unlike any outside of the armed forces and other first responder arenas.

Much has changed since *Fully Involved* came out. I still travel to various incidents for fire and law enforcement, providing critical incident debriefings, but I now teach more frequently and speak at various conferences. I created a couples workshop for first responder families, where I teach, and help them bond over, all the unique challenges we face.

Many fire departments throughout the United States have purchased *Fully Involved* in bulk for all of their employees, new and old. And while Jeff has always been well known in the Southern California fire community, he now enjoys also being known as the guy married to the woman who wrote the book. He's been on fire incidents where, when people have heard his name, they've walked over and said, "Oh, are you married to Mynda, the one who wrote that book? Are you *that* Jeff Ohs?"

It never ceases to please him when he's sitting around at fire camp, maybe at chow time, and the other firefighters want to discuss parts of the book. Sometimes there will be someone there who hasn't read it who asks what book they're talking about, and the others are always quick to respond, "Hey, it's his wife's. She wrote this book about us and relationships—you know the book."

And anytime the person says, "Oh, I've got to get that," Jeff never fails to note that he just "happens" to have some copies in the truck.

Our lives are full and busy these days. I continue to carry a full caseload while Jeff remains part of the fire service. Our contentment quotient is high; we have a good life, great kids, and the unique satisfaction that comes from being in a position to help others.

But we are not, and we never have been, perfect.

And by not perfect, I mean, we didn't start planning early enough for retirement. I suspect you haven't, either.

As a clinician who started seeing more retired first responders as clients, I became sharply aware of two things around the time I was finishing my first book. The first was that retirement issues for first responders and their families are far different from what others typically face. The second was that Jeff and I had long passed the stage where we should have started planning and that we needed to do so—and quickly.

Through planning together, we learned a lot of important things. We looked at our lives in a way we hadn't before and discussed where we wanted them to go next. We studied our strengths and weaknesses in the planning we had done. We spoke to our financial planner and sounded out our first responder friends who had already retired. We disagreed, we bickered, and we compromised on some things. And in the end, we felt closer to each other than ever, and we were also relieved to feel more secure about our future.

Some readers of my first book have said, both in reviews and to me personally, that, though fire-world-specific, they found *Fully Involved* to be a book that would be helpful to any spouse or couple in a high-stress, high-adrenaline career. While much of that book was specifically about what it's like to be married to a firefighter, I was happy to hear that others found it helpful, too. My clients come from all types of first responder sectors, so I was aware that many of them, and many of you who are reading this, come from other fields than firefighting. And when it comes to retirement, you have even more in common with each other than you do when you are working.

Relationships of first responders aren't like others, of course. Retirement isn't either. Most people face certain common challenges in retirement—boredom, isolation, financial worries, the feeling that their life isn't very impactful to others anymore—but for first responders, the logistics of retirement can also be very different. Retiring as a first responder is, in almost all ways, more challenging than it is for others. For one thing, first responders are like professional athletes. At any moment, they could suffer a career-ending injury, including PTSD. I'll talk about this in greater depth in Chapter Five.

Like any extended family, first responders come in all shapes, sizes, and callings, yet they have more in common than they have differences, especially when facing retirement. Retirement specifics and planning are almost identical for all first responders. Regardless of your specific occupation, you will be able to relate: the chances of working in the same area until retirement age or retiring due to stress, injury, or PTSD, exist for all. Are you a firefighter, a law enforcement officer, an emergency medical services (EMS) responder? Do you work in corrections, probation, or dispatch? Regardless, you are looking at pretty much the same scenario. If you're a firefighter, whether you work for your state, city, or county, or are employed by the federal government, you have more in common with other first responders when dealing with retirement than you have differences. The same goes for other categories; for instance, in law enforcement, whether you're a county law enforcement officer or a state highway patrolman, whether you're with a police department or sheriff's department, your challenges are more similar than different.

Like everything in our marriage, retirement is about both of us. And now that we're almost through with the retirement process, we have learned that it's a whole different ball game.

Whether you're married or single, whether you're the first responder or the spouse, the challenges you face were foremost in my mind as I wrote this.

Happily, this book, like *Fully Involved*, brought Jeff and I much closer together. As much as I work with first responders as a clinician, I always need input from Jeff. That's why I'm here: as with *Fully Involved*, I think my marriage and vocation come together so I can help others.

I want to help the first responder community as much as I can before I retire in a few years or reach the end of my life. It has motivated me how many people *Fully Involved* has made a difference to. I think and sincerely hope that this book will make a difference, too.

Due to the multitude of areas, it would take an encyclopedia to focus on every category of first responders, and I don't want you to be bored or overwhelmed. You will be able to fill in some of the blanks yourself because you have access to all of your department's retirement parameters. Most important of all, if you're not properly prepared—especially if you need to retire early—the consequences will be the same for you as for all first responders.

In the chapters to come, I'll share with you some of the discoveries Jeff and I made on our journey into the future. This isn't just our story, though. I surveyed hundreds of first responders, over 97 percent of whom said they would have benefited from more education on retirement throughout their career. But I didn't stop there; I went on to speak directly with a variety of first responders, as well as some of their spouses, about why and how they retired, what they did right and wrong, and what they discovered along the way that can help you and your loved ones plan for the future. Naturally, I asked Jeff how he felt about almost everything you'll be reading here. And even though I was the one bugging him to start planning, I understood his reluctance—and I understand why you might share it, too.

"This career path has been a major driving force in our lives for over thirty years," Jeff says. "It becomes part of you, what and who you are. Your family becomes part of it: you are a first responder family. It dictates so much of your life. During our careers, we tend to focus on the present.

"Because we get consumed by the career itself at times, we can lose focus on other aspects of our lives and family. So, to retire is like losing a part of your life, of your being. It requires a lot of change. We have all relied on others in our department and our crew, for our own lives in some hairy situations. We might not admit it easily, even to ourselves, but inside we know that retiring will leave a huge void in our lives."

This is true even for the closest-knit couples or families; it is so painful to think about leaving one's work family behind, many first responders just won't think about it. As a clinician who often works with first responders who are retiring or forced to retire, I know it's a delicate subject, but I also know it needs to be faced. About two years before Jeff hit his retirement age, I started bugging him, asking him what he wanted to do when he left the department.

That didn't light a fire under his butt to create a plan. He'd answer that "we will cross that bridge when we get there," which was, of course, not an answer at all, just what people say when they don't feel like discussing something. He had one of the retirement apps that are popular with first responders on his phone and was counting down the days until retirement. He looked at it all the time—so, naturally, I thought it was because he was excited. But when he hit that date and I asked him if he was, he just answered, "I still feel good, and I can still do the job." So, I left it alone most of the time, but I'd always get back on that train.

Finally, with thirty-two years in on the job and hitting his retirement date, he faced up to being ready to quit and said, "I'm on your time frame. When you're ready to start planning, we'll start." He started a master's program and looking at possible future jobs. I started thinking about both his retirement and the point when we would both be fully retired. We kicked off with a five-year plan and are now at year four. We're still working out the details, but we are being proactive. And, through finally making that decision, we have learned so much we didn't know before, information I want to share with you that will make you both more aware and more determined to plan your future.

If you didn't start planning or even thinking about retirement when you should have, don't feel guilty. You aren't alone. Not only are Jeff and I in there with you—most first responders are. I had over five hundred responses to my survey. Of those, more than 50 percent said they thought retirement planning should begin one to five years out. One year out? Not a great idea. Anything under five years is much too late for most people, unless they have been diligently saving and already have a very active life outside the job. About the same percentage of first responders had not yet discussed retirement with a financial planner, and this included a surprisingly large number with twenty or more years of service. Even more surprising—and one of the most serious retirement issues in careers that are high-risk for injury and post-traumatic stress disorder—over 70 percent indicated that they had no backup plan. *None. Nada. Zip.*

Here's the good news. No matter how much or how little planning for or even thinking about retirement you have done in the past, you can start improving your future life to come right away. It just takes some research and thought, a great deal of it pleasurable contemplation about the things you like to do most. I encourage you to share your ideas and feelings with your spouse, and some things with the rest of your family as well. Remember, you are a first responder family, a unit. Your spouse or significant other has shared so much more with you than what most couples experience, so this needs to be a "we're in this together" kind of thing for you to succeed. I was disappointed to find that only 23.81 percent of my survey respondents' spouses participated in their retirement plan. If you're young and single, you can bring your parents into the picture, to discuss things with them and make them feel included in your future. As you go along, you can start writing down some concrete plans and steps to take.

Trust me, I know first responders excel at functioning under pressure but are lousy at planning ahead. I live with it, right? But since they can do so under their pension plans, most first responders retire younger than the average worker. That means pre-planning is a necessity, as is planning for an unexpected retirement, which too many ignore until it hits them (sometimes literally) over the head. With the right input from others, I promise you that it won't be difficult or unpleasant, and will give you more peace of mind now and a better life as you get older. The best way to gain insight is always by hearing from people who have stood up to the same challenges, then discovering for yourself what works best for you.

I feel joy every day when someone tells me my first book changed their life, saved their marriage, lessened their stress and fight-or-flight responses, or made them a better parent. I hope this book will do something similar for you. Most of all, I hope it will inspire you to start planning now rather than "then." Doing so will give you a leg up and prepare you for retirement at any age and under any circumstances.

I am thankful to all the first responders, those still hard at work and those retired, for sharing their experiences and opinions on so many subjects to help you start pre-planning. You can learn from them how to avoid the pitfalls and stresses they faced as they were rudely awakened from their dream of a retirement that consisted mostly of sleeping late, doing whatever they wanted whenever they wanted, and not having to deal with constant emergencies—only to discover that they were miserable because the thrill of all that wore off quickly.

You'll find shared stories and advice on everything from the basics of planning to custom-designing a new life, from deciding where you want to live and what you want to do to learning how to manage overamped adrenaline responses. I've also included helpful checklists and advice on everything from controlling fight-or-flight responses, to deciding on possible new careers and hobbies, to exploring new states or regions you might move to and whether or not to downsize, to getting used to socializing with civilians.

Jeff and I do not possess any superpowers. As all of you will also do eventually, one day we'll wake up with no job to go to. We decided just in time that, when that day comes, we didn't want to be asking, "What happens now?" I want to help you, too, find your answers to that question before the fact.

We didn't start when we should have.

We didn't have a clue how much planning was involved and how much we hadn't considered.

And yet we are doing it.

And so can you.

PART ONE

When Will You Retire?

M ost first responders start out planning to be lifers. But that isn't always possible.

Feeling indestructible doesn't *make* you the Last Action Hero. Of those I surveyed, over 70 percent have been injured on the job; 56 percent of those who retired early did so as a result of physical injury; and almost 16 percent retired due to PTSD.

It is important to read each of the chapters in this section: Lifer, Injury, and PTSD. Why all three? Because not only does everyone start out planning to be a lifer, but even lifers who have put in their time can be taken by surprise and forced by illness or injury to retire before they thought they would. Of those I surveyed, almost 77 percent had no backup plan for that.

If you think I'm trying to scare you into planning for your future so you don't end up in trouble or seriously depressed, you're half right. I don't want to frighten anyone or make you shy away from planning your retirement. I do, however, want all first responders to follow the advice you spend your careers giving to others. Be prepared. If you are, you won't be caught off-guard and will be free to enjoy what can be the best years of your life.

CHAPTER ONE

My Life with a Lifer, and How We Got a Plan

My husband Jeff is a first responder through and through. His mind is on the job every day he's working. And on his days off, when he's back home again, he has never particularly wanted to talk about things like what needs fixing around the house—or what the two of us are going to do when he retires. Being soul mates doesn't mean thinking the same, and as a first responder, his first day off is always spent adjusting his Work Brain to Home Brain. But I am tenacious, so once I got it into my head that we were going to start planning his retirement, I wouldn't let it go.

Readers of *Fully Involved* related strongly to the "he said/she said" sections in the book, so when I started writing this one, I sat Jeff down, turned on the tape recorder, and got our planning journey—and struggles—down so we could share it with you.

We were on the lifer's journey: Jeff has reached his milestone and is free to leave and, while he's not out the door as I write this, he will be soon. Then we'll both continue to work for several years. Jeff already has some potential jobs lined up and hopes to find one that still works closely with fire, which is ideal for him. We are, in most ways, the average first responder couple looking at retiring after our financial goals have been reached, regardless of whether that means obtaining a federal, state, or city pension (CalPERS in our case), Social Security (since some departments pay into it), or a personal IRA.

Facing the Future

As we approached retirement, Jeff and I discussed everything—which doesn't mean we agreed on everything. But we tried to consider everything the future might hold.

MYNDA: What started me off worrying about Jeff's retirement was my work as a clinician. My practice was starting to see more and more first responders who were already retired or getting ready to retire, and they were not having an easy time of it. They were struggling emotionally with going into the next stage of their lives, and dealing with everything from nightmares to suddenly feeling unsure of their relationships. It made me think about us and the "plan" we had but had never talked much about in our twenty-six years together. Yep, over nine thousand days of not discussing the "Big R." For the first time, it struck me that we had no plan at all. Like Jeff, I had let myself slip into "figure it out later" mode.

JEFF: This was my life for so many years, I just wasn't eager to think about what came next. Plus, I was busy working with the department during a bad fire season, so I was home less than usual and it was easy to keep shrugging it off.

MYNDA: I started off by sharing some of the issues I was seeing with my clients and explaining why I thought we needed to come up with a plan, even a loose one, because I didn't want us to end up with the same problems. Jeff was not that into it, but he indulged me like the good husband he is. He does worry a lot about finances and being able to keep up our same lifestyle in the future. I worry, too, but because he was raised by parents who grew up during the Depression, his attitude isn't the same as mine; for instance, he's always looking at—and often worrying about—the financial aspect of anything. I respect that and understand his anxiety about committing to the next steps.

JEFF: Is there any of us who doesn't worry about money? Making ends meet and providing for our families is a priority for men in general, and certainly for all first responders, because our role in life is to keep people safe. So for me, envisioning not working means a portion of my ability to provide will disappear. That brings out a fear of the unknown, which for me brings out anxiety. I mean, who of us knows what the future will look like on a fixed income? We hear so many stories of retirees struggling from day to day. As first responders, we're fixers, so we panic at not being able to fix that.

We hear so many stories of retirees struggling from day to day. As first responders, we're fixers, so we panic at not being able to fix that.

MYNDA: I think all first responders and their significant others should be discussing retirement on some level as early on as they can. And I mean "They" with a capital "T." You both have to share—not every day and not so much in the early career stages, but you do need to put your ideas and dreams out there. For me, sharing also meant the opportunity to stay connected about our life together now that our children are grown up and our careers, at least the current ones, will be ending soon. Plus, since Kyle is a firefighter and Megan works in corrections, we can give them insight into what they should start thinking about while they're young and early into their careers. Once you start doing it, I think you'll find that it can be exciting and even fun to plan and take steps to save money and set up timelines.

JEFF: The fact is that, even though as first responders, we are planners to a larger degree than many—I mean, we have no choice but to plan our daily routines in a detailed way, to plan our days off and vacations in the same careful way—yet we fall short of planning our retirements. I wasn't surprised when Mynda showed me this in the survey answers. So, what the hell is wrong with us, planning everything except what many of us look forward to the most, which is not having to work? I want to see other first responders having this discussion early in their careers; I am making sure my kids do. This is a huge lifestyle change for us, probably much more so than for someone who works at a desk all day or follows a regular daily routine. And all we need to do is start planning, just as we do with everything else during our careers.

MYNDA: I think I can pretty much guarantee that you're going to start thinking about things you hadn't considered before. For me, the biggest challenge is Jeff being home all the time and making me his new hobby. In my first book, I talked about the loneliness and missing him, especially his not being home for the holidays. Maybe it sounds as if nothing will make me happy, but it's daunting to face all that togetherness when you've spent a quarter of a century figuring out how to enjoy being home alone and able to do whatever you want without anyone's advice or opinion. We have finally figured out a good rhythm for living together, now that we know we'll be doing it to a different beat.

JEFF: Our kids grew up with a lifestyle unlike other kids'. They talked about when Dad was home and when Mom was home or when both Mom and Dad were home. When you retire, so much about your life is going to be different that adjusting to being around each other all the time is critical. And it isn't as if a life of constant separations was so bad once we got used to it. Holidays at the station could be fun, and Mynda did fun things on her own or with friends. And even then, I remember her saying after the fourth day of a six-days-off period, "Can't you work a trade with somebody *now*?" or, "Isn't there any overtime you could take?"

MYNDA: As you go through these chapters, you'll read more about the threat of 24/7 togetherness and other challenges that first responders need to deal with in retirement. Some relationships don't survive it, just as some friendships fade away.

JEFF: It's something everyone needs to think about. That's the point. You spend thirty years having breaks from each other, and you make it work. Anyone who thinks it won't be a challenge when that ends is fooling themselves.

You spend thirty years having breaks from each other, and you make it work. Anyone who thinks it won't be a challenge when that ends is fooling themselves.

MYNDA: Also, a lot of first responders look at others who had to retire early due to injury or PTSD and think, "Oh, I'm so lucky. My retirement is going to be a breeze next to theirs." But I don't think a lifer necessarily has an easier time than someone who goes out early. Sometimes, it can be harder for, say, someone who planned to be a lifer but who changes jobs and moves to another state or a different division—perhaps by going from state to city or county. They might still think of themselves as a lifer, but they now have different issues with their pension, time put in, regulations, and a raft of other considerations. You'll be reading the stories of some people who have dealt with that type of situation, as well as those of many who retired as lifers while still in their fifties, with plenty of time to start a new career. The main thing is that you should always be planning—in every area of your life, from hobbies you would like to pursue to your dream vacation to what type of new career might suit you. You need to be able to adapt to changes in society, in your tastes and needs, and in the job. If your world has revolved around the job for many years, you may even have to relearn what it's like to interact with civilians. You may not realize how much your conversation has been affected by your career until you see the look of horror on civilians' faces when you start talking cavalierly about horrific calls you've responded to over dinner.

JEFF: One thing I've heard often is stories about divorce. The bottom line there has usually been that the couple did no planning or communicating. They may also have never addressed issues that already existed prior to retirement. Or maybe they didn't put enough time into the relationship and made it all about kids and the job and didn't realize they had grown apart until they retired and had to be with each other. A first responder retires, then picks up and moves to another state—and is divorced within a year. And, of course, we always have to keep in mind that we aren't "retire-at-65" people. Most of us retire younger. I'm in my fifties; I'm not about to sit at the end of a pier with a rod and reel. I don't feel old or even like I couldn't do the job anymore. I know I can be productive and give back. I still have plenty of life to live and I wouldn't even *consider* not having a second career. Even before I hit retirement age, I started teaching some classes to get the feeling for what it would be like to add some different routines into my life.

MYNDA: "Lifer" refers to time served, of course, so a lifer can still end up going out on medical or PTSD. Plus, because many couples are starting families later, we see people retiring at fifty with children under eighteen still living at home. I know quite a few first responders who have offspring from more than one marriage, so they run the gamut age-wise. That can be a big consideration in decision-making, especially if a divorced spouse moves to another city or state.

I can't stress enough how having some kind of plan is crucial to your retirement being successful, and I think that after you read other people's stories throughout the book, you'll agree and start planning intensely. It doesn't matter what your plan is so much as that you have one. It's easier to adjust your plan as things change than to start from scratch the day you retire.

JEFF: As you get closer to the date, I think you'll find that the job starts to de-layer a bit. You know, we see so much, and so much of what we see is not good. It's only natural to want nothing more than to move on with your life. Some people just want to get to the date and bail, and that date can't come quickly enough. If they have a solid plan, they're lucky because they can quickly move on to that.

MYNDA: But if they're not lucky, if they don't have a plan, too many first responders who just couldn't wait to get out have a rough time. They come to me for help with depression, alcohol and drugs. They weren't prepared to deal with retirement, so they feel discarded and obsolete and see a huge void stretching before them. That won't happen to you with proper planning. Not even if you don't make it to lifer status and need to opt out earlier.

Opting Out Early

Have you ever thought about opting out early? I know quite a few first responders who have or haven't done so after considering it. People have their own reasons for deciding the time has come to leave. I spoke with two first responders who left the job before they had planned to but not due to injury or PTSD. These people had figured on being lifers, putting in their time and retiring at the end of a long career.

Steve's situation was complicated. Due to an earlier departmental issue, he had moved out of his supervisory position as a captain in charge of fire investigation and gone back to firefighting. And then a new administration came in. "I had twenty-five years in," Steve, now well into retirement, recalls. "I was just fifty, but in many ways, I was mentally and physically done with the job. The administrative change finally convinced me. The fire department was downsizing, and we were taking a 15 percent pay cut plus having to change our schedules, the schedule I had worked for years, the only schedule I knew. I could have stayed in for three more years for an extra 8 percent at retirement, but there was a large payoff for leaving earlier.

"As soon as I heard about that, I went in the blink of an eye from thinking about it, to going to the pension people and finding out exactly what I would get, to literally coming in on my next shift and saying, 'I'm going.'

"I was heading to the whiteboard when I walked in, and writing '21' on it, with a circle around it. Everybody started asking, 'What is that?'

"I looked at them and said, "I've got twenty-one shifts left.' And every day, I'd come in, erase it, and change the number. So, I was ready."

The extra 8 percent had been tempting, Steve says. On the other hand, he admits, "Physically, I was prepared to leave. Mentally, I was over the calls. Sure, it was a shock, that total cutoff from my entire lifestyle. One day I was a fireman and the next day I wasn't. But I thought it was the right time. And it ended up working out well."

Like many first responders, Steve says he tried to plan but "when you're early in your career, you don't get a good grasp of what retirement might look like because it's so far away. I had some wiser veterans tell me to start getting into saving, even if it's just a couple of dollars a month. But I made some poor relationship choices that cost me money and kept me from sticking to a plan. So I didn't have a house that was paid off but one with a sizable mortgage payment. Still, I didn't retire with a bunch of bills, either, just that mortgage. And now I've resigned myself to knowing I will probably always have a house and a car payment."

The bottom line? When asked if he thought he had saved enough for his retirement, Steve was quick to answer, "No. Heck, no! What would I have done differently? Every time I worked overtime, I would have gone to the bank and deposited five hundred dollars. I would have saved more money. But retirement was pretty much thrown at me. I was planning for those three years, but then the buyout offer was made, I was told I had to decide in just days. When I realized I could live on what I would be getting, the decision made itself. Anyhow, money has never been a motivator for me, I don't earn it and burn it, but I don't want to die with eighty grand in the bank, either."

A Lifer Who Retired Twice

Life doesn't always turn out how we plan it. Wesley, a law enforcement officer from California, is a lifer who retired twice, once at thirty-one and later at fifty-one. After he retired the second time, he moved out of state. His experience has been complicated: positive in the long run but not so much so that he doesn't wish he had done things differently.

"My clock started at eighteen when I was a reserve, which doesn't count toward retirement, but I began working regular at a city department when I was twenty-one. I got injured at thirty-one and medically retired, but then I joined the sheriff's department and worked until fifty-one. So, it was a fractured career in its totality, but I never felt as if I'd retired; it was more as if I had just transferred from patrol to training. I didn't truly feel retired until I left California.

"I could have worked longer, but I ended up feeling burnt out. My last supervisor changed the dynamics of our department quite a bit. I could have put up with it, but I wanted to live in Utah. I left for the climate, the quality of life, and to be close enough to my grown children that my wife and I could drive to see them in a short time without a flight. Those things made my decisions easy as far as when to quit and where to go."

As far as his retirement planning went, Wesley admits, "A lot of what happened for me was flat-out luck. Ultimately, the way everything fell together, it looked like I was a genius, but it was a case of being in the right place at the right time. If I had to do it over again, I would have started planning a little sooner, but you get so caught up in the day-to-day life of the work that retirement never seems like something that will happen.

"I was smart enough to know that deferred comp and those types of things were important early on. In particular, when I started with the sheriff's department, I made sure that I had a deferred comp going, a percentage coming off the top of each check over the maximum period of time. But I didn't sit and work on a full-blown exit strategy until about three years before it was executed.

"Even then, I probably wouldn't have retired as young as I finally did if it weren't for my wife of thirty years, who worked on the plan with me. She's five years older than I am, and she'd worked for the state since she was a teenager, so she had over thirty years in. She was more done with working than I was and just wanted it to be over. We even discussed her retiring and moving on her own and my continuing to work with the sheriff's department for a few more years because the pension I would get from there wasn't anything substantial and we could have socked more away. But I was ready to leave. So, then we started focusing on where we would move."

You could say that Wesley's lucky streak started when he was retired at thirty-one with an injury and no backup plan but quickly found work he could do in spite of his injury. "It was pretty humorous because once I joined the sheriff's department, I'd have either Explorers or cadets go along on ride outs and tell me how they wanted to go into law enforcement as a career. Some would say, 'I plan on going to college and getting a criminal justice degree.'

"Every time I heard that, I'd give them the same sage advice, warning, 'Don't bother with a criminal justice degree because you never know when you're going to hurt your back, blow out your knee, or have something else happen that means you can't do the job anymore. And that criminal justice degree isn't going to help you anyplace. But if you get a business degree or something else that's transferrable, law enforcement as a whole doesn't care what your degree is. They're tickled to death that you have it. In other words, I'd tell them how they should plan their future, which was in direct contrast to how I had planned mine, since I had no backup plan."

Wesley has more to share—about finding a place to live, working part-time, getting used to being with your spouse, and finding things to do. He will be back telling you how he did it later.

It's Never Too Soon to Plan

You're going to see a lot more in these pages about backup plans because I consider nothing to be more important. "Have a backup plan" will be your mantra by the time you're done reading. And you *will* start planning. No matter your age, you will feel better when you do. And who could be better to back me up than a young firefighter and a juvenile corrections officer who just happen to be my children?

"Have a backup plan" will be your mantra by the time you're done reading. And you will start planning.

Our son Kyle was shaped by having a father who worked in fire. That helped him a great deal last year when he was injured on the job. "My parents' plan influenced me," he says. "Growing up in a fire family made me aware that one of the main traits of a first responder is making a little go a long way. Because of this, I made sure my secondary retirement savings were maxed out so most of the money was going into my savings. Then I got a second part-time job teaching so I can have a third retirement account and another source of income with the possibility of more work if I retire early.

"If you work this hard as a first responder for thirty years, the career takes its toll. Everyone deserves to relax and enjoy the spoils of their hard work, though some states make that harder than others. It all depends on the pension plans, which vary greatly.

"I never thought much about retirement until I was hired at my current CalFire department. It didn't really matter until I had found a place where I wanted to stay. Luckily, I had a lot of people through the years talk to me about retirement and give me advice, so I started now, while I'm still in my twenties. I want the best outcome and I knew it required planning."

The importance of retirement was driven home after Kyle's accident. He was not the cause of it; the fire truck he was getting back onto started moving suddenly without notice and he was thrown off, injuring him. "I thought the same way both before and after the injury," he says. "I learned early that this career will throw things at you. You could be perfect at your job and something bad can still happen. I've always tried to be ready for the unexpected, and I prepared for the possibility of retiring from an injury by instructing part-time at a college. If injured, I would do that and try to find another job that I would also be able to do regardless of an injury."

As a family, we are thankful that Kyle has made a full recovery, and Jeff and I are proud that he has planned better than so many who are older and more seasoned than he is. Our daughter also has a sound awareness of the importance of planning. "My thoughts about retirement were honestly in the back of my mind when pursuing a career," Megan says. "But I knew that I wanted to work in law enforcement, so I was aware that once I got into it, I could look forward to a good retirement plan. My father's plan and pension definitely led to my choosing a career that offered the same type. Retirement wasn't a big topic when I was growing up, but saving money was discussed consistently; I knew that saving up in case of an emergency was a must.

"I moved to Nevada because my husband lived there; I wasn't thinking further than that and the lower cost of living. Now I know that, in terms of retirement, living in a tax-free state will ultimately benefit me. I am glad to have Nevada PERS for my retirement, which will give me roughly 70 percent of my highest three years' earnings averaged out. The county will do that for the rest of my life if I retire as a lifer. I've also considered and looked into many other things that would affect my future: life insurance, health insurance rates in retirement, and where I want to be financially before I decide to stop working."

Growing up with a first responder dad and a clinician mom specializing in first responders has made both Kyle and Megan respect the importance of pre-planning. How great is that for a parent? It means Jeff and I can relax and enjoy our own retirement, knowing our kids will have good lives whenever they cease full employment, regardless of whether they turn out to be lifers or need to take that step toward their retirement unexpectedly. I know all too well that taking it suddenly and unprepared can be a disaster for first responders, as you'll see in the next two chapters.

Points to Think About:

1. Putting off thinking about retirement is not the path to a happy new life. If you haven't discussed all the different options with your spouse or significant other, this is a good time to start, whether your retirement date looms large or is far in the future.

2. There is always the chance you will need—or choose to—opt out early. That's a reason to be prepared regardless of your age or how many years you have put in.

3. You may not have to retire due to injury or PTSD but that doesn't necessarily mean your retirement will be a breeze when you start out. It certainly won't be if you haven't planned for it. It's not too early to think about changes you might choose to make and which I have written this book to cover: will you move, find a second career, work part-time at something new, travel more? And it's never too early to make sure you will be financially prepared to retire. Again, even if you now foresee your retirement happening far in the future, you should get some advice on putting part of your earnings aside for the future. And if you failed to do enough when you were young and retirement isn't far in the future, you should get the best advice you can from a financial expert who understands the pension plans and needs of retired first responders in your state.

CHAPTER TWO

Retiring Early Due to Injury

First responders think they're able to leap tall buildings in a single bound . . . until they crash to earth with a serious job-related injury. I get it, I'm married to a firefighter who has not once suffered an injury requiring workers' compensation. Jeff, who rushes into burning buildings and spends a good part of the hot, dry summers on duty at fire camp doesn't get hurt. On the other hand, I, his wife, contracted a whopper of a case of meningitis from working in EMS as an EMT and our son Kyle, who is always extremely careful, got thrown off the back of a fire truck when it took off suddenly just as he was getting on board. Go figure.

If you think you're immune to needing to retire early due to injury, that survey I did of over five hundred first responders has some news for you. Of those who did retire early, 56.10 percent did so due to physical injury. The next highest groups were those who suffered from post-traumatic stress disorder (PTSD/PTSI) (15.85 percent) and lifers who left due to a career change (15.85 percent) or family issue (12.20 percent). That puts the figure for forced retirement due to injury or PTSD at 71.95 percent of all first responders who leave the job early. Do you still feel indestructible?

First responders get hurt often. Only 19.3 percent of those I surveyed were like Jeff and have never been injured on the job. The other 70.7 percent have suffered a long list of illnesses and injuries. The most frequent are the ones we would expect: back, head, and limb injuries. But others have had issues with their hearing, hernias, job-related cancers and blood clots, accidents (most vehicular accidents for law enforcement officers in their patrol vehicles), burns, pulmonary issues resulting from fire exposure, dog bites, eye injuries, rhabdomyolysis (a toxic syndrome due to muscle injury), stabbings, and shootings.

When it comes to law enforcement and fire positions, back injuries are practically part of the job: police officers usually wearing twenty-five-pound gun belts twist their torsos every time they get in or out of their patrol cars, and firefighters tote sixty pounds of gear. Knees take a beating, too. Wildland firefighters are subject to injuries different from those of structure firefighters. Traversing rough terrains and steep hillsides, hiking often for hours at a time, causes knee and joint injuries while poison oak is a huge issue for any firefighter working wildland fires. Some firefighters, like my son, get hurt on fire trucks; if you're in law enforcement you may get injured taking down a suspect. For firefighters, a cancer diagnosis is practically inevitable; no matter what specific illness they suffer, it is considered to be a job-related injury. If you're in law enforcement, you're more at risk from stomach and colon cancer because your fight-or-flight response is so frequently triggered it keeps your food from being digested properly. EMS workers carry heavy gear and lift patients, both hard on backs and knees, while even dispatchers develop problems from twelve-hour seated shifts.

As a first responder, you're not, I know, a stranger to stress, no matter what your role is. And stress, we know now, is one of the greatest threats to our health. It can cause or exacerbate high blood pressure and strokes, digestive problems like IBS and Crohn's, migraine and cluster headaches, asthma, obesity, and mental health issues such as insomnia, depression, and addictive behaviors. Stress also exacerbates bad habits, such as smoking, overindulging in alcohol, and neglecting exercise. Not surprisingly, many police and fire departments have become very strict about any kind of tobacco use on the job.

As a first responder, you're not, I know, a stranger to stress, no matter what your role is. And stress, we know now, is one of the greatest threats to our health.

And, of course, research has shown that stress takes a toll on the immune system over time, leaving first responders, who invariably work close to others, susceptible to illnesses. A serious illness or injury can be devastating and can happen at any time. When Kyle was thrown off that fire truck, my first thought was whether or not he would be able to continue in his dream job. He's lucky, in that he can.

And, while my husband has always gone merrily along without suffering any serious illnesses or injuries, guess who got medically retired? Yes, me, due to meningitis I contracted on the job. Not only did I get sick but it's why I stopped working in EMS—which, as some of you know, is how I met Jeff. We responded to calls together when he was a paramedic, and I came down with meningitis not long after we started dating. This is also how I knew he was "the one" because he took such good care of me, taking me back and forth from the hospital and taking Megan to all her activities. Meningitis, an inflammation of the membranes that surround the brain and spinal cord, is a serious illness that can lead to death or long-term medical issues. It is so painful that I wouldn't wish it on anybody. I felt as if my eyeballs were going to explode out of my head; I was in the hospital off and on for a few weeks and out of work for months dealing with the long-term effects from the illness, so I couldn't go back. I struggled terribly with memory loss and couldn't remember how to get to the local hospitals. That's how I eventually became a stay-at-home mom until I decided to go back to school to get my bachelor's degree and then kept on going. So I know from experience how shocking it is to get a serious illness when you're young and healthy.

A firefighter I know named Joe was totally unprepared when, at age twenty-nine, he was diagnosed with esophageal cancer. "I was the guy at the fire station who made sure people didn't smoke or chew tobacco fewer than a hundred feet from the entrance," he says. "I was always telling them, 'We're exposed to enough crap; you don't need to be doing that, too.' And then there I was with cancer.

"I ranked number three on the captain's list before I got diagnosed. Just a couple of months before my diagnosis, I'd been told I was getting a LT [limited term] captain's job at a different department and the chief would be coming to give me my badge. So, I took myself off the list. They still let me be a LT captain, but I took myself off the permanent list so I wouldn't block anyone else. And in that year alone, they hired everyone in ranks one, two, three, and four. So when I came back as eligible, I reinstated as available, and they more or less said, 'Pick where you want to work because you're so high on the list, we have to give you a job.' So I went in as a permanent captain at a station."

Happy ending, right?

"Almost a year after moving to a different station," Joe says, "I walked past my chief there, and he said, 'Joe, why are you walking funny?'

"I said that I didn't know but that my legs felt weak and I'd have it checked out. And he said, 'Cool. Take time off and go get it figured out.'

"They diagnosed me with ALS, amyotrophic lateral sclerosis, which most people know as Lou Gehrig's disease. Then they decided it wasn't ALS. I took every test they could throw at me—spinal tap, EKGs, one after another—and they couldn't figure out what it was. All they could say was, 'We know it's not

ALS because you're still alive.' They thought it could have been caused by the chemotherapy or radiation or even by the cancer itself.

"Everyone's advice had a common denominator of 'You're lucky to be here. Go live your life.' But obviously, that meant the end of firefighting. In my state and my area, they don't have any administrative positions you can be in; you must be ready to work on a fire engine if needed. That meant there was no position I could fill as a captain that didn't require a physical I knew I would fail. So I had to tell my chief that I wasn't coming back."

Like anyone who goes out on injury, Joe didn't retire right away but went out on disability. "Finally, the state came to me and I was told that if I couldn't come back to work, I had to retire. I tried everything I could to stay on the job. I said, 'Put me in the command center, put me in training, put me somewhere, let me do something. I'm only thirty-three years old!'"

But Joe had no choice. If he couldn't work as an active firefighter when needed, he had to go. He medically retired due to cancer, which was covered by workers' compensation, which meant that all subsequent treatments and diagnoses he received could be tied to having had cancer—including this motor neuron disorder in his legs, which was likely caused by the cancer, chemo, radiation, or all three. After he medically retired, he says the illness got worse quickly, then it leveled off and has remained more or less the same for the past seven or eight years. He's more active now and works out to stay fit, but he says that the more he does and the harder he taxes his muscles, the more it sets him back.

So here's a guy who's forced to retire in his early thirties. And did he have a backup plan? "Absolutely not. I started as an Explorer at sixteen. Then at eighteen, as soon as I could, I got a seasonal fire job. I was going to college then to try to get my degree because that was a big thing with my parents, but working seasonal fire doesn't mix well with college. Anyhow, I was set, so I decided I didn't need it. I was pretty close to my associate's degree, but then I got a LT engineer job and I just thought, *I'm good. I'm on my path. I don't need college.*

"Now my dad's warning of 'You need something to fall back on, something to rely on in case anything happens' haunts me. I had a little bit of education and a degree in fire. I knew everything about fire. And, of course, back when I started and was promoting, a degree wasn't a big issue. It was how good you were at your job that counted. I know a degree is more important now and some people are doing it on the job. But you have to do it. Someone young might already have decided to be a first responder for their entire career, but, still, for any upward mobility, you have to have that degree. And there I was, going, *What the hell am I going to do now?*"

Starting Over After an Illness

You'll be learning more from Joe later as he shares what he learned about building a new life as a former first responder. For all the hardship he went through, he was luckier than many because his department was supportive of him every step of the way and he never felt abandoned. His first department was a small one, with about twenty stations, that he describes as truly being "like a family." When he got promoted after his cancer treatment, he went to a large county department with hundreds of employees. "In a big department like that, you're more of a cog in the wheel, which is both good and bad," he says. "There's a lot of opportunities, good call volume, and all types of calls.

"The issue is, a department that's so big can be impersonal. I was lucky because the partner I worked with was the brother of the battalion chief, so I still had that family feeling. And the department took care of me. Everything was fully covered. And the people were great—all my fellow employees, from the captains to the engineers. Before I retired, I was off for so long that

I burned through all my sick leave. We had a time bank, and I had *years* donated to me by others. They'd just say, 'Hey, Joe, you can have a month of my vacation time.' It allowed me to be out longer, and it went well, with everything covered."

Like every retired first responder I spoke with, Joe wishes he had known back then what he has learned since. "Nobody thinks about long-term care," he says. "When you're a first responder, you're like Superman, thinking you can do anything and nothing is ever going to hurt you. Now, I would tell everyone they need to have the what-if plan that I never had. I thought I was going to be a fireman for my entire career, even after the cancer treatment. I thought I was going to end up running the department.

"You have to have that mentality because you're a different breed and you have to believe that you are the best at what you're doing. You have to think that you're always going to make the right decision. It's almost bred into you. And the funny thing is that if I had known more back then, I wouldn't have done it. I appreciate everything that I got to do: work on a helicopter, a ladder truck, a squad, but—

"When I was fifteen years old, the father of a friend was a county fire captain. One day he said to me, 'Joe, what are you doing with your life?' I was fifteen! He said, 'You're going to be a fireman.' And I thought, *All right, that sounds good*, and I became an Explorer. And that's how I ended up on this path."

Even though Joe says he wouldn't have become a first responder if he'd known then what he knows now, he has no regrets about the life he chose, as it led him to the life he has now, with work that he enjoys and a wife and family he loves. "When I got cancer, I wasn't sad or feeling sorry for myself. I was angry. I've never been a 'things happen for a reason' kind of guy. When I got cancer, my parents went full-bore religion, and they truly believe—and I think it's awesome they do—that God healed me and I'm still here only because of that. But again, being a fireman and coming up in that world, I take some credit for what I achieved. Otherwise, if things are going to happen for a reason, why do we try? Why did I study so hard? Why did I become an engineer at twenty-four years old? Why did I work my ass off?

"So, is there a reason I got cancer? When I was going through it, there wasn't a reason why I had cancer. There wasn't a reason why I had to retire. But if fifteen years before I had to retire, someone had come to me and said, 'Hey, Joe, you're going to lose your house, you're going to lose everything, but here's where you're going to be in fifteen years even though you will have to go through hell to get there,' I would sign on the dotted line and do it all again."

Through learning the hard—maybe the hardest—way, Joe has very firm ideas about what first responders should do to be prepared. If he had started when he first became a permanent firefighter, retirement at thirty-three still wouldn't have been a breeze, but it would have been less painful. "Have a plan B and plot out your future," he advises. "We can't dictate what's going to happen, because who knows what it might be? As far as on-the-job things go, I would say to do everything you can to keep yourself safe and healthy. You need to be your own advocate. Whether or not it costs you money out of your own pocket, you need to do what you can to stay healthy, because your health is more important than the job, and if you don't protect your health, the job will take it from you."

Health is something young first responders can be very cavalier about. Even my son sometimes says he's going to die of cancer anyway so what does it matter? This is a more common thought than the average non-first responder would think or believe. My response has been to Kyle or any other young first responder, "Yes, your chances are much higher than a non-first responder but you can also do things and behave in a way that will decrease your chances and odds. No need to just throw caution to the wind." As a mom and a wife, I'm here to remind all first responders (and that includes my son) that, hey, you are *not* invincible, and taking care of your health should be a top priority.

Joe's advice to others? "Don't let the job be your whole life. Being a first responder doesn't dictate who you are. At the end of the day, it's a job. You have to realize and accept that. You have to—because one day you'll walk away from it. I still have first responder friends, of course, and when we get together, I'm like, 'Dude. I don't care about all the overtime you worked, I'm over it. Do people who work at Burger King talk about flipping burgers when they sit around the campfire? Hell, no. So, have a life outside the job. You need to do other things and have other interests. They say that once you're a firefighter, you are a firefighter twenty-four hours a day. If needed, sure, but that doesn't mean you have to wear the uniform all day every day. Never forget that being a first responder doesn't determine who you are. You were who you were before the job and you'll be who you are after you retire."

Never forget that being a first responder doesn't determine who you are. You were who you were before the job and you'll be who you are after you retire."

"Almost" a Lifer

Ethan was sixty-two and worked in EMS for a private company. If you're a young first responder, please read that statement from Joe again about the drawbacks of working for a large, private ambulance company. As most of you know, working for a private ambulance company isn't the same as being a city, county, state, or federal employee. For one thing, the pay is low, closer to minimum wage than to what a fire department paramedic takes home. For another, the benefits aren't much better than the pay.

Not that Ethan was worried. He had just three more years until he could retire and collect Social Security. Then, as he says, "My vision of working until sixty-five got upended. I couldn't keep working."

When we spoke, Ethan was still trying to quickly plan his future. He wasn't having an easy time facing up to the harsh reality that serious back and joint issues—degenerated disks and arthritis caused by the work he did—meant he could no longer physically keep doing his job, and that he had no reliable safety net. There was no way he could work, as his physical problems meant he was no longer up to doing a medic's requirements. His doctors told him he could end up paralyzed.

All of you know how hard it is to be a first responder out in the field, loaded up with heavy gear. It's even worse for workers like Ethan, who needed to be able to pick up patients, often carrying them up or down stairs, and have to lift about eighty pounds of necessary gear out of the ambulance. As his health issues grew, Ethan felt continually more let down by his employers, but determined to keep working if he could. He also felt betrayed.

"They don't value people enough," he says. "They're making millions or more off the time and effort of their employees. We are the face of the organization; we are who people see when they call for help. As one of my professors at paramedic school once said, fifteen board members are raking in millions of dollars in these private ambulance organizations, but it's the people who are performing the services that earn that money for the company, and those people need to be taken care of through health benefits, through seeing their job end.

"First responders are like professional athletes in that neither of these groups hold jobs for life because physically, it wears them down. And employers are saving money as a result of the benefits that employees who can't make it to the end will lose."

Ethan had always wanted to be a medic. "I was a junior in high school when *Emergency!* was on TV," he remembers, "and

I thought, *Wow, that's a pretty cool job.* It was fun and exciting. They did some amazing things. And they did medicine. That was important to me because one of my ancestors founded the school of medicine at a major university. To keep the tradition alive, I knew I would choose either EMS or veterinary medicine. But getting into vet school was a lot harder.

"So, I became an EMT, working in our local hospital district during my junior and senior years of high school under an ROP program. My coach's wife was a charge nurse and tried to talk me into going into nursing, but even though I considered that a valuable career, I wanted to be playing with the big toys outside. So, first I became what was then called an ER tech for two years. In 1979, after I graduated, I went to paramedic school. In 1980, I started with an ambulance service. I moved onto a larger service after that and then another major private ambulance company. I've been a paramedic over forty years, forty-five if you throw in my EMT service."

In other words, when you're young, being an EMT sounds like such an exciting and worthwhile endeavor that you don't mind that you're not making much over minimum wage. You don't mind that you're not offered a retirement plan or that you have no pension. The only way ambulance workers get a pension is to start their own IRAs. When I spoke with Ethan and his wife Lori, Ethan was still out on worker's comp but about to retire on disability. "About fifteen years ago, my company started offering 401(k) plans, but they weren't putting into the plans as a private agency, so they weren't bringing as much to it as they'd said they would. They said, 'We're offering this for your retirement,' but they weren't backing up the words with actions. I was young and newly married to my first wife, and there were other things in my life that I needed to put money towards, so I just didn't think I should bother with it.

"Another ambulance agency came in and bought them out and they finally turned the words into action, so for every dollar we saved, they were matching it by 6 percent. That's when I joined the 401(k). I still couldn't put a lot in because I didn't make enough working for a private agency."

In many ways, Ethan had a good career. It was something to throw himself into when his first wife died after a long illness. Besides his actual duties, he devoted time to teaching, being a field liaison, or acting as a representative for the teaching agency. He was also a representative at EMC conferences and with the county EMS agency. He became what his second wife Lori calls "the guru of EMS," a teacher much in demand for paramedic students. After they married and had children, Ethan continued working hard. And he paid the price. "I was pushing my body too hard," he says. "In my belief, that's what created all my medical issues." Those medical issues led to Ethan himself needing an EKG, but the chest pains he was having turned out to be stress-related and not a cardiac problem. That stress—caused by forcing himself to work and his fight to keep the company from forcibly retiring him—finally convinced him the time had come. By the time you're reading this, he will have fully retired, thankful that, for all the things he should have done but didn't do, he did at least open that 401(k), which will allow him to get by until his Social Security kicks in. He's lucky because, while many first responders don't get any Social Security depending on their department, his Social Security will start paying out early due to his being medically retired and will help him and Lori live out their dream retirement at last.

Right now, Ethan is still working on his plans. When I asked him what he knows now that he wishes he had realized sooner, he said, "To start a retirement plan earlier. I still believe this is a wonderful career. You have to love this job to do it and you need to be a people person. I still can't imagine a job where I'm stuck in one room. But it comes at a cost. Every job has its problems, but problems that are manifested by the administration shortchanging people in the field and by the healthcare system, that's the biggest issue I see. It gives us the greatest grief due to the pressure they put on us as individuals being the face of the organizations we serve, whether public or private."

The bright spot here is that Ethan finally came to terms with being forced to retire, and he has made his wife happy by now being there 100 percent for her, their kids, and their grandchildren. I'll be bringing their story back later when we look at how retirement affects spouses and planning for the future. In the meantime, if you have former first responders among your friends who left due to injury, just ask them what they regret the most. Some will say it's that they didn't just stay in bed on the day they ended up lifting one piece of gear that was too heavy or whatever else caused their injury. But most of them will admit it's that they just didn't prepare or have a plan B.

And don't think you can just sit back and rely on workers' compensation, either. One of my patients, an ambulance EMT, herniated two disks in her back, and nine months later, she had still not been contacted about her physical therapy. And when she complained, they told her to lose weight. She said, "I know I'm overweight, but I've been waiting to be told what I can and can't do." And there is plenty you can't do if you have herniated disks and are overweight. But this is why people often try working through their injuries. Not to mention that addiction to pain medication can become an issue when people are trying to push themselves to ignore severe pain and need meds. And in any case, the stress of being injured is often compounded by the stress of being forced to go back to work.

It is difficult for any first responder to retire, because their identity and their every waking hour has been so tied to the job. It's harder to retire with an unexpected injury than it is to retire as a lifer, and many of the challenges are different. In most states, it's even more difficult to retire as a result of mental health issues. But no matter why or when you walk away from that life, the best cure is prevention—in this case, preventing a situation where you've lost that job and have no plan for what comes next. As long as you do that—plan—you will be able to enjoy the relaxation and freedom that comes with your well-earned retirement.

Points to Think About:

1. Never let yourself think you're exempt from having to retire due to an injury. It happens, sometimes in the line of duty, sometimes from a health issue that starts small but worsens over time. This is especially true if you work in an area that requires you to lift and/or carry heavy equipment. Are you prepared?

2. You can't plan on sitting back and living off workers' compensation because it's not that simple, and it can be an exhausting battle to get what you deserve. The same goes for your department: they will not necessarily come to your rescue. You were hired to do a specific job and if you can no longer do it, they won't jump at the chance of finding something for you that fits your health or injury issues.

3. You have just read the experiences of people who hadn't prepared enough. They could be you. The best step you can take right now, for yourself and your loved ones, is to start saving for a rainy day that could come at you out of the blue.

CHAPTER THREE

Retiring Early Due to PTSD

While almost 16 percent of the first responders I surveyed said they retired early due to PTSD, the numbers are probably higher. One of the reasons for this is that many of them were certain they had post-traumatic stress disorder, but in their state and department, it wasn't yet recognized as grounds for medical retirement. It still isn't easy to get a PTSD diagnosis, and once you do, the process is still long and complicated, from starting a workers' comp claim to seeing doctors with no guarantee the claim will be accepted. It's much more difficult than in the military, for instance, where PTSD has long been accepted. Some first responders just threw in the towel and left to find another line of work. Some of them didn't even allow themselves to admit what was wrong but just kept going as long as they could. There was a lot of pressure to just suck it up and stop complaining. There were no standards for many years, either for diagnosing PTSD in first responders or recognizing it as an accepted and necessary reason for medical retirement. And it wasn't as if someone with one bad call too many could just see a clinician and get support; many clinicians weren't equipped to help those who needed it. Of those who told me they had seen clinicians, the reviews were very mixed as to whether or not it helped. I'm glad to say this is getting better, but having more culturally competent clinicians will make the process more successful for first responders.

Everyone faces stressful moments in their life, but nothing compares to what first responders deal with on a steady basis. I wrote at length in *Fully Involved* about how firefighters—and this applies to all first responders—have to confront stresses that can push them past burnout into compassion fatigue and post-traumatic stress disorder. In the relatively short time since I wrote the last book, PTSI (post-traumatic stress incident), which was once considered a post-traumatic state of short duration, has now been accepted within the first responder community as a synonym—and perhaps will one day be the preferred term—for PTSD. There are two reasons for this: PTSD is becoming accepted as a job-related injury, especially since research has shown more and more that it causes physical changes in the brain, and also because the use of the word "disorder" is considered by some to imply that the sufferer is at fault. (There is also the term "acute stress disorder," which is applied if the condition lasts fewer than thirty days.)

Whatever anyone chooses to call them, states of ongoing high stress are red alerts. They can put a first responder's mental health on the line, with suicide being a possible outcome. A white paper on Mental Health and Suicide in First Responders, based on a study by the Ruderman Family Foundation, found that, in 2017, at least 103 firefighters in the US committed suicide, compared to ninety-three who died in the line of duty. First responders are likely to suffer PTSD at a rate *five times* the national average.

Many fire and law enforcement departments are doing more to help identify and provide services to help those afflicted, but adequate behavioral health programs are far from being universally in place. Still, if you ever experience any symptoms of PTSD, you need to seek support; if you ever feel suicidal or capable of causing harm to yourself or others, you need emergency help. You should always have a list of available first-responder-specific resources and can request this from your department or if you have a peer support team, they will have all the resources.

This chapter is about retiring—by choice or by being forced out—due to PTSD. This doesn't mean that if you're a lifer or just decide to walk away and find another career at age thirty, you will not suddenly be haunted by memories of bad calls or be woken by nightmares. Those possibilities aren't uncommon and I'll be sharing information about them later. The most important things to keep in mind about PTSD, and this is true in every case, are: it is a work-related illness/injury, it is not your fault, you are not weak, you can learn to manage it and learn to live with it, and you are not alone. There are many resources available to all first responder communities. Reach out and don't try to go through it on your own.

Recognizing PTSD

There is a great deal of information out there regarding PTSD, including in *Fully Involved*, my first book; in talking about retirement, I want to quickly go over the symptoms, because if you have symptoms of PTSD, you must seek counseling and support. PTSD might not be the culprit behind your emotional struggles, but four criteria of a diagnosis of PTSD are listed below.

- **Intrusive thoughts:** (at least one symptom in this category) these can include flashbacks to the traumatic event or nightmares. PTSD also tends to cause emotional or physical reactions to things that remind you of the event—driving down a street that reminds you of where you were during the incident, hearing a noise that sounds like shots fired, or simply smelling an odor associated with a bad call.
- **Avoidance:** (at least one symptom in this category) you try not to talk or even think about the traumatic event, and you may avoid doing things, going places, or seeing

people that can bring back memories. Drugs and alcohol can easily become avoidance crutches.

- **Negative thinking and depression:** (at least two symptoms in this category) you may start having bad thoughts about yourself or others while feeling things will never get better. You can start feeling detached from your family and friends, as well as things you once enjoyed, or you might feel numb and find that you are not experiencing things on an emotional level. Your ability to maintain close relationships can fade and you may have trouble remembering things.
- **Changes in physical and emotional reactions:** (at least two symptoms in this category) your arousal symptoms are not what they were before the incident. You might become easily startled, frightened or always on guard, more so than you are in standard Work Brain mode. You could find yourself responding aggressively or angrily in a way you didn't before or behaving in self-destructive ways such as driving recklessly, drinking heavily, or using drugs. Both your ability to concentrate and your sleep patterns could be disrupted.

To be diagnosed with PTSD, the condition has to have lasted consistently every day for thirty days or more and must impair daily functioning. You must exhibit the precise number of each as listed above. If you fulfill some but not all requirements, you might be diagnosed instead with acute stress disorder; this can last three days to a month and is diagnosed based upon experiencing nine or more symptoms in any area or areas.

Diagnoses are tricky because PTSD is measured more subjectively than objectively. There has always been workers' comp, and physical injury is more easily measured. There are criteria for going out on injury, and a doctor can point to a test and say, "Statistically, this person can never go back to work at this job," or, "This person will need to take six to eight weeks off." Physical injuries are measurable, which makes things easier. If you draw out your time off, you can catch a lot of grief, but you pretty much drop off the radar and it takes a good year or two to get you medically retired.

But with PTSD, things aren't easily measured, and, unlike in the military, there is no difference in degree. You are judged to be suffering from post-traumatic stress disorder or not, period. In the military, the percentages are based on what is known as the General Rating Formula. They will give you a percentage of disability from PTSD, such as 50 or 60 percent, based on the average of your mental health symptoms. And if you are diagnosed at 50 percent or less, you could still get a regular civilian job without being hampered by the diagnosis. In 2020, the state of California passed AB542, declaring PTSD a presumptive injury, which makes it a work-related injury. However, as it now stands, there are no guidelines or framework, so it's a gray area as far as what gets accepted in individual cases or not.

Also, you can be diagnosed with PTSD and feel able to come back to work but be forced out medically. So much depends on what state you're in that it would take an entire book just to address that. Not all departments and not all states have gotten on board with viewing post-traumatic stress as a work-related injury. Many are moving that way, and it's going to get to the point where every state has, but some are still holding out.

Doctors aren't sure why some people get PTSD and others don't. But it is not a sign of weakness or something that should cause shame and elicit a refusal to acknowledge how you're feeling. As a first responder, you are in a career that can trigger PTSD at any time, as well as re-trigger episodes of PTSD by putting you in situations similar to the original traumatic event. I wish I could say that this all goes away when you retire, but it doesn't, and I'll be discussing this reality and how to deal with it later. Just be assured that, if you ever have to quit working due to PTSD: (1) it is not your fault, and (2) it is a job-related injury and you deserve the same retirement benefits as anyone else due to a physical injury or illness.

What often happens is that someone who had undiagnosed PTSD or was determined to have recovered from PTSD and banished their demons retires as a lifer and the PTSD suddenly rears its head. That can happen as the brain relaxes out of work mode. And those who are still working find, often without being fully aware of it, that their symptoms are under control more when they're working because they're more on alert, so rather than deal with the symptoms, they sign up for more overtime and work more, which is not a wise path to take. Please don't ignore or deny disturbing triggers whether you're active or retired. You can be helped.

PTSD Always Catches You by Surprise

Jim was only two years from retiring after what would have been a twenty-five-year career with the same department when he was forced out due to PTSD. He says, "I've come to believe it was the perfect time to retire. I was fighting it tooth and nail at the beginning, but I think it was what God wanted, and I stopped fighting that."

Jim went through all those years of working for the fire department without PTSD, and then, as often happens, it suddenly struck without warning. "I was in a classroom training atmosphere at the academy," he recalls. "The first week, we were going through PTSD information, the signs and symptoms, and I thought, *But I feel kind of like that at times. And I kind of feel like that right now.* Then we went through some scenarios, and it hit me hard. It happened in an instant for me.

"I didn't know what was going on; I felt as if I were out of my body in that classroom. I couldn't concentrate. I couldn't even think. I was a wreck."

As soon as Jim returned home from the training, he told his wife what had happened. "She got me to the right people through EAP, the Employee Assistance Program," he says, "and I saw my first counselor, then I went to a trauma retreat. Now I recommend everyone go to a retreat, even if they're just feeling down or have only a few symptoms."

Though he could have stayed on with his fire department, the reassignments would have been non-safety. He couldn't get reassigned to a non-field position; that news gave him severe panic attacks just thinking about being on an engine and having to run a 911 call. So, he chose not to stay on. "It would have been a completely different retirement and it was not what I or my family wanted."

Jim wasn't totally unprepared for retirement, being so close already. Unfortunately, he hadn't decided he should do deferred compensation until he was at the mid-career point. "I didn't think much about supplemental retirement before that," he admits. It was only at his wife's urging that he kicked their plans into overdrive so they could be comfortable and have a backup plan. Like many first responders who retire, especially when it hasn't been foreseen, he had two children under eighteen. "I was planning to retire once they were out of high school," he says, "but, obviously, things changed. Now we'll just support them until they become adults. What's great is that being retired, we're going to be able to do a lot more things with them than we were able to when I was with the department. That's neat, especially considering all the times that I missed Christmas, birthdays, and other family events."

Despite being somewhat prepared, Jim still wishes he had done more financially, regardless of whether he had retired early or not. "I think all first responder departments and agencies need to provide more education about retirement from day one," he says. "Things have certainly improved. Back in the early nineties, no one spoke about retiring. I was just another boot fireman who didn't think about those things. I wish I would have had a captain or someone else early on who had coached me, which is what I did for others as the years passed. And retirement in general was still hard for me because I wasn't ready and I was dealing with PTSD. I got through the transition with the love and support of my family, and with the wise words from my therapist."

The PTSD didn't magically go away when Jim retired. Even with clinical help, he had to deal with flashbacks that he hadn't had when he was still working—and sometimes these still return to unnerve him.

Soon after he retired, Jim got a part-time job delivering pizzas in the neighborhood where he had grown up and worked as a first responder. He expected it to help occupy his mind and keep the flashbacks at bay, but that didn't work. "Just driving around town delivering the food, I would turn a corner and suddenly think, *Oh, that's where that dead person was*. Or, *This is where the lady got hit*. It wasn't out of control, but I kept having small panic attacks. I hadn't even considered that this would happen. And it was part of the reason we eventually decided to move out of state. I needed to get someplace else, somewhere new and refreshing."

Not only did Jim change locales, he also sought help. "I learned a lot from seeing a clinician and going to a trauma retreat. Now I have the tools that help me calm myself. I would say my retirement was more of an emotional struggle than anything else."

I think trauma retreats should always be offered and that it's good to have something similar at the end of a first responder's career regardless, just to help with the stresses of retirement and the chance of possible flashbacks. They do something like that in the military. When someone returns from a deployment, they go into a special program with a social worker to help them in the transition period. The same thing would be a great benefit to our first responders. As a first responder, you have had a certain mindset for years. As a practicing culturally competent clinician, I think it is invaluable to have assistance in learning how to switch out of it and how to deal with old calls that are still stored away in your brain when they pop up.

Jim went through a four-day retreat. "But even if it's just two or three days," he says, "something that leads to desensitizing or deprogramming your Work Brain would be helpful to everyone."

One thing we have discovered is that you don't need to have experienced PTSD on the job to have those bad moments when you retire. So many first responders are shocked when they retire because they didn't anticipate any of the bad things coming back like that. But calls from twenty or twenty-five years ago do resurface. Remember, PTSD doesn't just go away. Jim has had others talk to him since his retirement, telling him about their own experiences. "One of my bosses told me, 'I have calls, too, that I should have taken care of a long time ago.' It's good to have a list of clinicians on hand so you can talk to someone if you need to after you retire. Guys tell me all the time, 'I went through it, and I'm getting better, but I still have it. I have a lot of unresolved things that come and go.' I always suggest they talk to a counselor or go to a trauma retreat."

When Jim and I spoke, he and his wife had recently moved and he was about to change his health insurance plan. It is important to always know what your insurance covers, especially if you have retired and aren't yet on Medicare. What coverage do you need? Are you checking policies for mental health services and coverage? Some first responders can find extended insurance through their Employee Assistance Programs and get authorization just before they retire so they will be covered for six months after their retirement date. But departments often don't tell them that.

I asked Jim if he had any advice for younger first responders about feeling symptoms of PTSD, and he told me, "I think it's important that if you have a problem, you talk to your coworkers, significant other, or a counselor about traumatic calls and events that you have or had in the past. You need to get through all those bad calls and tell someone else about them. We think we're super tough, but we're not. One of my last chiefs said to my wife, 'I never thought in a million years that Jim would be the guy to have PTSD. He was always so happy and joking.' I also advise younger workers that they need to start planning for retirement and have a backup plan as soon as possible in case of anything unforeseen."

Because a serious injury or PTSD is always unforeseen, that means everyone needs to start planning when they're young. As we saw with Joe, even a debilitating illness can pop up without warning. Jim told me he never asked himself, "If this ended today, what would I do?" It can happen to anyone. He was fortunate in that he had done most of the right things financially and that his wife and his faith gave him strength and helped him start to build a new life. Here's a guy who can now calmly look back and say he retired at the perfect time, even though it was rough and he felt deeply let down by his department.

While money isn't the only challenge faced by first responders who don't plan, it is the one that can be most easily planned for throughout your entire career. Sure, you will still have to deal with the other issues involved, all of which we'll be looking at next and all of which every first responder leaving the job will face. But you will be more able to deal with those challenges and settle into true contentment, whatever that looks like for you, if you don't have to worry about the basics of survival.

Points to Think About:

1. PTSD is a work-related illness/injury that isn't your fault. It is a mental health condition that results from trauma and is not related to strength or weakness. There are many resources available to first responder communities that can help you

learn to manage PTSD and live with it. It's important that you don't try to go through it on your own. PTSD is recognized and accepted now, and you can move forward whether the result is your returning to work or retiring.

2. As a first responder working in a stressful and often dangerous environment, you owe it to yourself to be fully aware of all the signs of PTSD so you can get help. You will be able to see a clinician and go to special workshops and retreats that can speed up your healing and trauma management.

3. Even if you end up retiring because of PTSD, your life is far from over. You can have as good a retirement as anyone else, whether you find a new career or decide to take it easy for a while. But, again, because it can happen to anyone at any time, this is one reason first responders must always be doing what they can to be forward-thinking financially and prepared for whatever lies ahead.

PART TWO

The Things You Didn't Think About

Here's the thing about a new life: it needs to be built. It isn't going to be delivered on a silver platter. It will be chockablock with challenges, from being a full-time significant other to dealing with the signals you receive from your still-active Work Brain to figuring out just how the heck you're supposed to be spending every day for the rest of your life.

These are key reasons for planning far in advance and laying down your retirement foundation before the big day arrives. It will be different for everyone, of course, but most responders tend to believe they are going to find retirement an endless vacation. In reality, if you don't prepare ahead of time, it will be more like being grounded at the airport when all the concessions are closed, silence surrounds you, and you have no thoughts on how to amuse yourself—or worse, no idea how to convince yourself you're still relevant to the rest of the world. The excitement is gone, replaced by feeling bored and insignificant. Now is the time to be proactive.

CHAPTER FOUR

Home Sweet Home

Even for first responders who were yearning to retire, adjusting isn't easy.

Those fantasies of sleeping until noon and having hour after hour of free time can wear thin pretty darned quickly as the reality of spending day after day with no solid strategies, few plans, and a spouse on hand 24/7 sinks in.

Not surprisingly, spouses know better. The majority of first responders I surveyed, 42.19 percent, were looking forward a great deal to retiring. Those significant others? Only 32.44 percent of them were looking forward to their first responder becoming a retiree. Even more sobering, while only 5.47 percent of the first responders were not looking forward at all to retirement, 11.37 percent of their spouses (twice as many!) were not eagerly awaiting the day—not even a little.

That's the challenge of being a first responder's significant other: they put in a great deal of time learning to get by just fine without their partner being on hand for important anniversaries and events until, *bang*, the reality of full-time togetherness looms ahead and even those spouses who had been looking forward to their first responders spending more time with them aren't thrilled—and it's not a walk on the beach for their first responders, either.

First responders retiring now are struggling more than those who entered the workforce within the last five years because the mentality of being a first responder has evolved. For those who recently retired or are close to retirement, the mindset was that the longer you're in fire or law enforcement or any other responder role, the more often you give the job your everything and choose career over family. Now I watch my son and other younger people, and the difference is striking. They aren't being told that the work should be your everything, that it is your life. They are being encouraged to have balance in their lives, and that's a huge improvement. Current lifers have more to deal with because the absence of their former life will often be felt more as a loss than as freedom and also because they will not have built up as much of a life outside the job.

The first thing both retirees and their significant others will need to deal with is "thereness." I am not used to my husband always being there. As a lonely stay-at-home mom, I realized early on that I needed to make my life fulfilling even though Jeff wouldn't be there for much of it. Through going to school, getting my bachelor's, master's, and doctoral degrees, I came to appreciate my independence. When Jeff was gone for days at a time—weeks if he was on a fire assignment—I kept busy, not just with my kids but with friends, especially other fire spouses. I was used to designing my own social life and enjoying my freedom. Now, I'm getting used to having Jeff around much more. And sometimes I'm still terrified, and I know many significant others feel the same. It took us all these years to get comfortable with being alone and figuring out what to do with our free time, and now that we're used to it, we have to turn it all around. I also believe that the saying "Absence makes the heart grow fonder" is true. When Jeff was gone, I missed him. I had things to tell him when he got home, and I was excited to see him. I joke often that I believe our marriage worked because he wasn't around all the time to get on my nerves.

The first thing both retirees and their significant others will need to deal with is "thereness." I am not used to my husband always being there.

It might sound minor to those who haven't reached this point, but let me tell you, having all the stuff that annoyed us before in our faces every day now doesn't make our hearts go pitter-patter with joy. It drives me over the edge to hear someone always saying, "Why are you doing that? We never did that before." And my husband is *that person*. Jeff will want to do everything for me and then I have nothing to do. I fear I will become his hobby.

That's one of the things we started talking about as soon as we started planning. We talked it through—recounting how when we were together too much we could get on the other's nerves—so at least we got a head start on figuring out how to work out whatever comes up. If you've read *Fully Involved*, you know that Jeff and I can both be pretty hotheaded and strong-willed but we both learned to speak candidly then. Now, it wasn't so stressful to be open in telling each other what possible issues we foresaw before the fact. During the edgy times, family members will need to stop, breathe, and think, *Well, we've been in it a long time, so why start over now?* Then you just work it out. Marriage isn't easy for anyone. I always ask my clients, "Why do you think marriage vows are so intense?" It's because marriage is no joke and not just something that happens or works out. It takes work on it every day till you die. Communication is always the key, and it's important to deal with your communication skills long before you get to the retirement phase.

Whether you're a first responder or a significant other, you need to make a plan with your spouse and, sadly, not enough people have been doing this. I had expected my survey answers to be high regarding how many first responders' significant others did not participate in the retirement plan, but I was shocked when 76 percent of those who responded said their significant other hadn't participated. Seventy-six percent! Think about it: you are about to switch to being with this person every single day, but they aren't even invested in your planning. If you're doing this as a first responder approaching retirement, think about how you're setting up a whole dynamic of surprise that is not good for your relationship. No wonder so many spouses aren't excited about their first responders' retirements! Maybe it's time to take a good look at the quality of communication in your relationship.

I don't know if many female first responders behave as the men do when they're planning to retire. I think a lot of men figure, *It's my retirement so why would my significant other care?* or *Nah, she's probably not interested.* They don't consider how much it's about their spouses' lives, too. They just assume it's about them. And then they become the problem because they don't think about anything but how great it will be to lie around or go fishing and not have to stick to a schedule. But retired first responders without a solid plan are the ones who become needy. Their significant others are used to planning their free time.

Togetherness is the hurdle and the preventative care for it becoming a burden is, as always, planning. And that will be different for you and your family based on your interests, your lifestyles, and the family itself. If you have kids still at home, your plans will not be the same as if you're empty nesters like Jeff and me. If you're alone, your plans will be different. This is going to be your life from now on, so you want to make sure you plan it well.

*Togetherness is the hurdle and the preventative care
for it becoming a burden is, as always, planning.*

How Full Is Your Nest?

When a first responder retires with kids still at home, the situation is very different from an empty nester's. Jeff and I, as the latter, will be spending more time together than we ever have. Now that we have moved to Las Vegas, we're able to spend more time with our kids. My daughter and her husband live nearby and my son, while still commuting to his firefighter job in California, has his own apartment even closer to our new home, so we can all be together more often as a family. For me, there's the added boost of being able to do mother-daughter things with Megan. We go to the gym to work out, go shopping together, meet for lunch, and so far have been having an all-around fantastic time being geographically closer. And, yes, it's still early days.

Some empty nesters also have grandchildren, and that often opens up a whole new life for them if their extended family is nearby. It can also be a pain in the butt if the couple isn't into being babysitters, but many retired first responder couples are thrilled to be helping their children out plus spending more time with the grandkids. Regardless, you need to make sure your kids know the boundaries for grandparenting. As Jeff put it, "If you're going to do grandpa daycare, you'd better have an idea of what that looks like and what it may come to if grandpa says, 'I'm done with this!'"

While there's more pressure on empty nesters not to crack up from being stuck with each other so much (just kidding, Jeff), having children still at home can also create stress and conflict. Because our first responders have been out of the picture for so long, they may carry a burden of guilt for the fact that they had to work rather than spending more time with their kids. This can lead to overcompensating and overinvolvement. Trying to make up for all the times they couldn't be there can lead to two different approaches—on the one hand, overparenting by being critical and demanding, on the other, becoming "Disneyland parents" and smothering the kids with affection and giving them anything they want.

Divorced parents with young kids often have it much better than when they're working. Most first responders are very involved with their children or try to be, even if they're divorced, and retirement gives them the freedom to spend more time with the kids even as it frees them from arguments with their ex about being forced or having to work overtime and also means they can be home every night for dinner.

The tricky thing if you're divorced is not feeling resentment if your former spouse is getting a sizable chunk of your pension. It's also something to take into consideration when planning because many times a first responder will work longer to make up for the retirement income they lose to an ex. But the important thing, married or divorced, is being able to spend the second half of your life with your children and grandchildren. That's a cause for gratitude.

Whether your children are young and still living at home or older with their own lives and families, your relationship with them needs to be considered when you plan your retirement. If they're adults, how close do you want to be with them? If you're divorced and remarried, with a second family, would you prefer to spend more time with your first family or concentrate on your current one?

Challenges of the Single Retiree

What if you're a single first responder moving into retirement? It won't be a big change in some ways—you won't have someone in your home every day who belongs there but who can some-how seem like an interloper or a guest who's stayed too long on what was supposed to be a week's visit—but being single pres-ents challenges as well. Many first responders haven't explored the dating scene at all. If you're unmarried, perhaps you're newly divorced or have a casual relationship that satisfies you and feel no need to play the field.

But it's just as likely that you settled into a routine with your work family that blunted the need for anyone else. This is es-pecially true for firefighters, who physically live with their fire family much of the time. But it also goes for every other category of first responder, not only because of the close bonds forged by working in lifesaving and often life-risking jobs but also be-cause work simply came before everything else. So that feeling of bereavement, of losing an entire way of life with nothing to immediately replace it, can be devastating.

As for dating, it might be a far different scene from what it was when you last paired up. Dating apps have changed the MO, making meeting people easier in some ways but creating new problems. After all, it's human nature for people to exaggerate things online, so you don't always get what you were promised. Some of the first responders I spoke with said they ended up connecting with too many people who had heard or read a lot about first responders ending up with big pensions and seemed interested more in money than in a relationship. Some just got burned out by the endless cycle of "perfect matches."

So, how do you meet potential romantic partners when you retire? Whether you're thirty or fifty, it's a challenge. For retired first responders, particularly those who have few outside inter-ests or hobbies, the easy answer can be hanging out in bars. Did I mention how many first responders develop alcohol problems, especially when they retire? Alcoholism and drug use are serious issues for first responders everywhere. It's both easy and tempt-ing to start dropping into the neighborhood bar for a few beers every day or evening. You get social interaction with no ties, friendly yet detached servers, and always the possibility of meeting "the one." But it also offers endless alcohol and, especially if you choose the club route, a lot of drugs on demand. And it's easy for that "occasional" shot of Jack Daniel's or a quick joint shared in the parking lot to become a way of life. Add boredom to the mix, and you've got the perfect scenario for excessive drinking.

That's one reason to find things you once liked or would like to try and to develop hobbies, as I'll discuss in Chapter Seven. You're more likely to meet the right person at a golf course, art class, or campground than at the local bar. And, yes, you need to make an effort. We'll be looking at interacting with regular civilians later in the book, which will help you whether you're looking for love or just trying to make friends. Remember, the "new normal" for you is what's accepted as the plain old regular normal for most people. You'll need to relearn some skills. but it will open up a new world for you and get you out of the house and into building your new life.

How Much Togetherness Is Too Much?

Even the most solid relationships suffer stress when first responders retire. Again, retirement is challenging for everyone; life remains the same for few couples. And for first responder families, the stress is exacerbated. You might be moving to a new area. Perhaps you will decide to sell your existing home and buy a smaller one, even if you don't leave the area you live in. You may retire with medical or psychological issues that pile on the stress. You might grow depressed because you looked forward to this day arriving but now that you're retired, you feel bored and irritable. You could feel betrayed or hung out to dry by your department. Your significant other might be frustrated trying to deal with your feelings and moods. They might resent having to give up the freedoms they had when you were gone all the time and you might now resent that they built a great part of their life without you, the part you used to not be around for. One way or another, you might just work each other's last nerve.

Remember Lori and Ethan from Chapter Two, Ethan whose progressive back injuries from his EMS work eventually forced him to retire? They are an amazingly devoted couple. But it is still taking them some time and patience to get used to their new normal.

"The routine we'd had since we were married shifted because I was used to having two days where he was at work for twelve hours and it didn't matter what I ate, what I was doing, when I went to sleep, or how long I'd be watching TV," Lori recalls. "Now that he's around more, he's noticing and commenting, and I finally said, 'Shut up. You never used to notice that. Just leave me alone.'

"It's because the routine we had for so many years was one in which he always won except when we were on vacation. But then by the time we would *be on* vacation, I was like, 'When are you going back to work?'

"So we're relearning how to be all the time, which was always the plan, but in our case, it was so abrupt and not a choice. The phone rang and someone said not to come in the next day. And he still hasn't gone in to get his stuff. Part of me wants to say, 'If we're done with that, you need to go to the station and get your stuff.' But we want to figure out the next part of our life first."

I think every spouse finds having a full-time housemate trying at first. Mary is the wife of Jim, who talked about his anxiety and PTSD in Chapter Three. They had already gone through a lot together before he retired and she has been his biggest cheerleader. As a spouse, she found his retirement easy to take—as long as she was working herself. Things didn't change until she recently joined him in the ranks of the retired—about two years later. And even though both were retired firefighters, the transition was challenging. "When he was gone, with both of us working, I just held down the fort and made everything happen. I ran the whole system," Mary says. "Then, when he went off on injury and I was still working, he was home all the time managing the house and taking care of things. The only thing I did was pay the bills. He did everything."

Not surprisingly, this meant that now there were two people committed to doing that "everything" in their chosen ways. "So I've got my system in place from before, but now I'm messing up Jim's system. I tell him jokingly, 'You're micromanaging me!' Still, we had to figure that out. I had to admit that it had been his space for a long time since being off on injury and that he'd been the one holding down the fort while I was gone. So we had to figure all that out and relax. Now it's good. But sometimes I think, *Please don't let him ask me one more time, 'Can I get you anything? Do you need anything?'* It's sad for some because not everyone has the same relationship we do. When someone's first responder retires and I hear about them splitting after retirement because they can't figure out that being-home-together-all-the-time part, it breaks my heart."

Mary and Jim found that having children still at home when they retired helped. "Our teenaged son was playing football when Jim went out, so he got to drive him to football camp and watch the games and do all the things he had missed for so long. It's so important for a boy in high school to be involved with his dad. And our daughter, who's a bit younger, is happier, too. Having their father be here for those moments when they need him is huge. I'm thankful for how it's all turned out." Even though Mary had planned to work until her son graduated, the challenges Jim faced due to his PTSD changed that. "It was a hard year," she says, "and it burned my bulb out quickly. That's when we started talking about it, and we ramped it up and made the change."

Because they worked together to smooth the tradition, Mary says the couple is relaxing into their new lifestyle. "I enjoy not having to set an alarm clock and letting the dogs wake me up instead. In the mornings, we just hang out and have our coffee, and since we have only one car, we go everywhere together. We're thinking of taking on small part-time jobs to keep busy, but we have truly worked it out. The process is weird, and I think the biggest thing is being supportive of each other and being prepared for the huge change in your home environment. If someone is a stay-at-home spouse and their first responder is going to be home all the time, that's going to have a big impact on them. They need to prepare.

"And if that spouse is a company officer or chief officer, they might be expecting to be the boss all time, and I can see that being an issue. Again, you need to be open to talking about what you see as problems. One thing I've seen is some wives not getting that because their first responder worked with women, they will probably remain in contact with those women after retirement. I think significant others need to learn how to deal with that."

It's important to discuss and set boundaries as to what you're each comfortable with, keeping in mind that it's unfair to expect a first responder to give up friendships with the opposite sex; this is particularly true for women because as first responders, most of their friends tend to be men since they will have worked with men more than with other women.

What if your significant other is also a retiring first responder? Won't they understand all the issues? Not necessarily. Wesley, who spoke in Chapter One about his early retirement, is married to another retired law enforcement officer. "There was definitely a difference in the volume of time we spend with each other. With my wife also being in law enforcement, we had the whole ships-passing-in-the-night scenario. It was great back then getting to hang out for a couple of days when our days off matched, but then we got thrust into being with each other seven days a week. That changes the dynamics. Now our new home has my office completely isolated from the rest of the house. I typically go into that office between eight and nine in the morning, and my wife might not see me until three or four o'clock. And she gets six hours or so to do her own thing without having to worry about what I'm doing."

Because they moved from California to Utah, the couple were experiencing their new normal in a new house in a new state with new things to see, which Wesley said helped. He did start his own travel business as well as working part-time for the local sheriff's department, which keeps him occupied and gives him time to study or read while his wife, "a huge fan of retirement," spends a lot of time taking care of their large property and garden. Having their own interests and spending much of each day on their individual routines, Wesley says contentedly, makes them appreciate their shared time on the weekends.

As a retired first responder, you need to be patient if your spouse doesn't see the new normal as "normal" at first. While a significant other might be like a radar gun in clocking friendships you have with the opposite sex, they might not be at all aware of the grief process you go through in losing that work family. Many of them don't anticipate the phase of depression that often accompanies leaving the job behind. They can say things like, "How can you not be happy to finally be retired? We've been looking forward to this for so long!" A lot of significant others don't know how invested you've been or understand your sadness. I've even had spouses tell me, "I don't care about their career, and I don't want to hear about it."

As a retired first responder, you need to be patient if your spouse doesn't see the new normal as "normal" at first.

That's not going to work for anyone who lives with someone who has spent a majority of their time with their crew. As a first responder who will retire one day, you can help ease the transition by making sure your significant other is aware of the bonds and understands the depth of your engagement with your coworkers. As Mary told me, "You truly do have two families, and your spouse has to be accepting of that."

Even as a clinician, it was hard for me knowing I would soon have Jeff wanting to have more input than he had while working. Even with all the effort we've put into working through any issues, at this point we're both still a bit cautious. Jeff worries that he'll bore me, and I worry that I'll get under his skin by not doing things the way he'd like but the way I've always done them when he's working. Then again, Jeff didn't marry me because I was docile but because I always knew and spoke my mind. So, in our transition, in pushing Jeff to retire and in making moving plans, I grabbed the reins.

He was having freak-outs about retiring and moving to another state. His unease and conflict showed themselves in his not being able to make any decisions—this from a man used to making life-or-death decisions every day! So, I decided on my own and put our house in California on the market without getting any confirmation from him. I knew that if I didn't, he would hem and haw and keep saying things like, "Well, you know, we can look . . . or we can . . ."

And it would never have ended or turned into "We'll cross that bridge when we come to it."

It freaked him out, but I was up-front and said, "I'm sorry, but it wasn't out of disrespect. It was that I knew you weren't going to call it." So, I gave him a kick in the butt and from that time on, he was excited about our plans. I'm not advising any other couple to take drastic steps, but I know my husband well and I knew the time had come for me to just go for it and that Jeff would understand. When I tell anyone, even other first responders, that I did this, they all cringe and say "Oh, man! Gosh!"

I want to help you make changes and make a plan, too. That's what this book is about. One of the things you can start doing right now is talking and dreaming, not just about sleeping late or not having to check in, but about what you would genuinely like to do with all the free time on your hands, where you might choose to live next, second careers you might consider, whether you want to buy an RV or travel more in general. It is never too early to plan. And the more you plan together, the more you share what you'd like to do and what you worry about, the more prepared you'll be when the day comes. Talking and dreaming together can strengthen and even rebuild your connection with each other—and your "Home Sweet Home" will end up being sweeter than ever before.

Points to Think About:

1. You and your significant other are not used to togetherness around the clock day after day. Make sure you don't try to either run things or avoid things but do give each other some space. Don't try to be the boss, but aim for a strong partnership.

2. Retirement is a major change for everyone, so if you're single, make sure you have a support system and friends to spend time with. You don't need to avoid dating apps, but be aware there will be disappointments. And single retirees shouldn't rely on nothing but bars, clubs, or Tinder and Match.com, either. Get involved in events and groups that interest you and will lead to meeting like-minded people.

3. Retirement is a great time to get to know your family better—to spend more time with the kids and grandkids, to see the world with your significant other, and to build stronger relationships. As with everything else, being successful at these requires open lines of communication and a willingness to share and to try to understand points of view and feelings that might not match yours all the time.

CHAPTER FIVE

Work Brain Doesn't Retire
So Fast

One of the many things first responders tend to ignore or not even be aware of before retirement is that, especially in the beginning, Work Brain keeps functioning and shoving Home Brain out of the way. This isn't unusual: after all, Work Brain saved your life, making you hyperaware and ready to react quickly to any threats. If you read *Fully Involved*, you probably realize already that the Work Brain/Home Brain split *drives your family crazy*.

When you're in Work Brain, stressful situations—a disagreement with a neighbor or family member, worry over finances, being cut off in traffic, even a sink backing up—can get stress hormones pumping into your bloodstream, causing physiological changes. Even non-first responders are familiar with that sudden heart-pounding reaction to stress as the fight-or-flight response kicking in.

Ask most retired fire responders and they'll tell you they still check out a restaurant when they walk through the door: where the emergency exits are and if anyone is acting a bit wonky, as if they could be trouble. That's only natural. "I don't think you can ever totally let go of who you were and are," Jeff says. "This has been my life for thirty-four years, and it isn't going to suddenly go away. Being a firefighter is a fun job in many ways. For me, there will always be a draw to a big fire, and I know there will always be a pull towards that excitement.

"The same goes for Work Brain. It will be hard to let it go since it's been a part of your life. Repetition has made it a part of who you are and how you act. I doubt it ever goes away completely, especially for law enforcement. But you can learn to avoid places that look like there could be trouble and let yourself relax as much as possible. Work Brain is no longer a necessity."

When working, you need to stay in fight-or-flight mode. That goes with the job description and not knowing when an emergency is going to spring up. So, when as a first responder you arrive home from the job, it's natural that you would still be in Work Brain mode. That can cause you to have a sharper sense of being alive and laser-sharp attention. But because you're flooded with adrenaline, you're in *biological* overdrive. There is only one way for it to go when you go home and crash into Home Brain: down into irritability and exhaustion, which can make you hypervigilant and hypercritical. It's why at our house, when Jeff would come home from working for several days, both the kids and I felt like we were waiting for an inspection as soon as Jeff walked in the door.

When you retire, it isn't as if you just flip a switch and the brain split ends. Little habits die hard and sometimes not at all.

Work Brain Affects Retirement for All First Responders

The Work Brain/Home Brain issue affects you regardless of what type of first responder job you have or had. The difference lies in the shifts worked and recovery time between those shifts. If it takes eighteen to twenty-four hours for the body and brain to biologically shift out of Work Brain, then those used to working eight-to-twelve-hour shifts have rarely been out of Work Brain in their career unless they've had several days to go on vacation.

That significantly impacts their ability to show emotions other than anger or irritation. Cops have a higher divorce rate than military or fire. Some cops can't shift out of Work Brain, causing them to lose their humanity or empathy for others, including their own families. Unlike fire departments with specific areas to cover, ambulance and EMT workers often cover entire cities and get moved around as calls come in. They might never get a break during an entire twelve-hour shift. Most private ambulance companies have stopped twenty-four-hour shifts, but it's still a twelve-to-fifteen-hour day.

It affects you when you only get to go home and snatch a few hours' sleep before going back to work again at a high-stress job. Being a dispatcher might seem easy to those unfamiliar with the job, but the rest of us know that working a twelve-hour shift where you never get to see anything, but just listen and talk instead—making sure you stay calm and never letting your voice fluctuate—intensifies your sensitivity to voices and any fluctuation in tone. This can make you more critical of friends and family if you sense a negative tone or attitude. As a dispatcher, if a mother calls in screaming that her baby is drowning in the pool, you stay on the line until help arrives, then hang up—so you won't necessarily get closure on the call.

Corrections workers have a unique challenge: they must never let their guard down because an inmate could sense vulnerability and attack. Seeing criminals get privileges they consider undeserved can stoke anger and resentment, and the feeling that they have to work hard to survive while the criminal gets it all for free. No matter the job, some similarities carry on into retirement: a need for control, easily stoked anger or resentment, attention to detail, a "my way or the highway" attitude, and demands for information. As I said, when my kids were young, the night before Jeff would come home from his shift or a fire assignment after being away for at least a few days or a few weeks, I would begin the night before secret ritual and go over the list of what had to be accomplished—rooms cleaned, everything put away, some tasks around the house—everything that needed to be completed before Jeff walked through the door.

When the kids ran in to say, "Mommy, we're all done!" I would do an inspection. For Jeff's homecoming, everything had to be perfect. Whenever he did come home, we were all happy. But he rarely had more than one foot through the door (okay, maybe he made it all the way to the kitchen) when I'd hear his ominous sigh. He had found the one thing I missed, rather than the hundred things I didn't. I worried that he wasn't happy at home. Otherwise, why was he always laughing and joking whenever I called him at work? It wasn't until I got my PhD that I realized the culprit wasn't me, but the hypervigilance required on the job.

As a first responder, you've been used to coming home and taking eighteen to twenty-four hours to come off the adrenaline high and the fight-or-flight response. Work Brain is operational, task-driven, and without emotions. That's the survival mechanism. But if you don't plan a transition routine for retirement, you will deal with your new life from a Work Brain perspective because it is more comfortable and less messy with feelings.

If you don't make a smooth transition from Work Brain into Home Brain when you retire, the issues in your personal life will be the same ones your family had to deal with while you were working. It's hard to have a loving conversation or caring conflict resolution with a spouse or child if you're not connected to your feelings. You can come off as too matter-of-fact or even abrupt or insensitive. I continually hear spouses telling me "He (or she) is here physically but not mentally."

So far, Jeff and I haven't been having the fights we used to have when he was working. Back then, I knew Jeff wanted to help and be a part of the family when he came home—but we'd still end up fighting because he didn't want to do every single thing my way. The same will probably hold true for us in the future, but since we dealt with it before, we know how to make it work. That doesn't mean we have it all figured out or that we don't fight. Many think that because I do this for a living that I have it all figured out and we don't. What we have changed and learned was how to come to the table and have a healthy conversation about the issue, which these days are mostly to do with annoying each other or disagreeing on things. And I admit that I still storm off at times, then shut down and refuse to talk.

Work Brain Active Duty Versus Work Brain Retirement

Here's a chart that will help you foresee and deal with the changes between being on active duty and being retired. Perhaps the most important habit in having a successful retirement is self-awareness. If you become and stay aware of Work Brain/Home Brain challenges that are a particular struggle for you, you can work on them and manage their power. Mind you, these aren't all the issues, and they aren't the same for everyone. This is just a way to boost your awareness and understanding of how the way you think can affect you in retirement.

ACTIVE DUTY

Win or Lose mentality: As a first responder, losing meant that someone's dying, a house or property is being destroyed, or you get in trouble and risk losing your job.

RETIREMENT

Win or Lose mentality: This behavior at home isn't about such severe situations. Instead, it can cause you to overreact to your family, resulting in defensiveness, excuses, and feeling attacked. You need to work on not reacting to challenges or disagreements as if each one was a life-or-death situation.

TIPS:

- Talk a deep breath and listen.
- Ask for clarity.

- Use "I feel" statements to express your feelings.
- Don't try and fix every problem.
- If you feel attacked or angry, ask for a time-out, calm down, and return to the situation.
- Don't have a serious conversation through texting.

ACTIVE DUTY

20-second fix: Scene time and response times were critical to the job, which had time-sensitive situations that could mean life or death for you or the community you served. Also, the facts were all that mattered, because there was no time for small details or feelings.

RETIREMENT

20-second fix: You will not be dealing with many, if any, life-or-death time-sensitive situations. It's time to take it easy. You'll still be prepared to act quickly in an emergency, but you need to focus on defining whether something is urgent or not and then acting appropriately. This applies to when your family or significant other wants to discuss their day or a situation that's upset them. It's easy to want to rush them or push for the facts as if you're in an interrogation. It will take practice to slow down and listen to a longer version of the story without getting frustrated.

Tips:

- Remember that other people's brains don't work with just the facts or scene time.
- Read books or listen to podcasts about cognitive behavior therapy (CBT) to learn how to change your thinking.
- Take a breath and listen.
- Remember your family hasn't had you around all the time and may want to talk more frequently.

ACTIVE DUTY

Controlling behavior: Being in control of your safety and others was your first priority. Scene safety and keeping your head on a swivel were beaten into your brain for your safety as well as that of others on the scene.

Overprotective: You saw the worst things possible day after day. This caused you to fear for your family constantly even when you want to have fun. It may also have made you have trust issues and ask lots of questions.

RETIREMENT

Controlling or overprotective: Your skills as a first responder aren't needed in most situations now. Because of your career, you will always be somewhat controlling and overprotective, since you can never unsee or unhear the things that are stored in your head. But you can retrain your brain to act this way less than when you were active.

Tips:

- Have patience with yourself and others while you are adjusting your thinking.
- Find things to keep you busy and prevent you from overthinking.
- If you feel anxiety or fear about a situation, perform a small task to distract your brain.

ACTIVE DUTY

Hypervigilant: In your work, you never knew what danger might be lurking around the next corner, so you were always on the lookout and poised for trouble. Your brain and body were in constant fight or flight mode. This made you hyperfocused, energetic, funny, and alert.

RETIREMENT

Hypervigilant: Relax, okay? You needn't keep checking the door or trying to suss out everyone in the room. You can be aware without going overboard now. And you don't need to worry, because you will still be better at spotting possible dangers than the average person. Some behaviors will never go away, including sitting so you can see the door, knowing where all the exits are, noticing weird behavior. The goal here is to retrain yourself and your brain to bring it down a notch. It may take some time to not always be on alert but, with practice, you won't always be poised for trouble.

TIPS:

- Don't wait for this to go away on its own; it takes intention and practice.
- Utilize more coping skills to manage your anxiety about the changes in your life.
- Create a schedule for yourself so you have control over something.
- Practice expressing your emotions and fears to your family; I promise they will understand.

ACTIVE DUTY

Everything to everyone: You were needed and felt needed. For your entire career, you tried to not let anyone down, whether it was your coworkers, family, or the community. You had a purpose in your life.

RETIREMENT

Everything to everyone: You will always be valued—perhaps even more so now, because you'll be valued as the person you are rather than the job you do. You will still be needed, but now you will be able to accept and embrace your own needs more easily.

It will take an adjustment to find a new purpose and meaning. You will have more mental space now, because you won't have to worry about letting your coworkers down. You may feel the urge to worry more about your family, trying to make up for lost time.

TIPS:

- Remember your family and spouse knew what they were getting into. You don't have to make up for anything.
- Hobbies or a part-time job will help with this, as will volunteering and getting involved in community groups and projects.
- Don't take it personally that your family is independent. Remember, they had to be, and it will take time for them to adjust, too.

ACTIVE DUTY

Regimented schedules: You had no choice, and the schedules weren't always to your liking, but they shaped your life and created some order to the chaos. You even began to crave it.

RETIREMENT

Regimented schedules: You can still make and stick to schedules, but they don't have to be as regimented as before. Scheduling in retirement is a good thing. It will help you wake up every day with a sense of purpose and course of action. Scheduling your days is especially important when you first retire and might feel lost without a definite daily or weekly plan.

TIPS:

- Don't try and schedule the whole family; they don't need it or want it.
- Write your schedule out on a calendar or whiteboard, as it will make you feel productive.
- Schedule in fun and self-care.

- Schedule dates with family and friends.
- If you want to change something in the house, sit down with your significant other and discuss it like a team. Keep in mind that they have been the ones running the household.

ACTIVE DUTY

Separated from emotions: This is a survival skill for dealing with a career of trauma. It allowed you to see the bad parts of the world. However, it does become difficult to reconnect to those emotions and requires more energy than you may have at times. How often was it drilled into you not to let your feelings interfere with the work at hand?

RETIREMENT

Separated from emotions: This is the most important challenge and one you *must* attend to. You have stored and ignored an entire career of horrors. They will come back to the surface in dreams or intrusive thoughts. Don't let it scare you or take you by surprise. Just because you have retired doesn't mean you're a regular civilian. You don't need to dismiss, ignore, or keep your feelings bottled up now. Talk to people about how you feel: your partner, friends, or a clinician. Most retirees need to seek professional help for a short time while processing the slide show in their heads. Being able to tap into and express your emotions will help you understand both yourself and others, and improve your outlook and relationships.

Tips:

- Seek professional help from a clinician even if it's short-term.
- Participate in a trauma retreat.
- Read, research, and listen to information that will aid you in experiencing your emotions regularly, as this can be overwhelming overwise.

- Consider couples counseling or workshops to learn how to be with each other daily.
- Learn some new communication skills that work better with civilians.
- Learn and use "I feel" statements.
- Talk to other retirees about the dos and don'ts of retiring.

Working Out the New Normal

The situation for retired couples isn't hopeless, but it helps to plan ahead. Retiring will require a big adjustment for both of you, as well as your children if they're still at home. If, like John and Mary, you were both working and then one retired while the other continued to work, it means making necessary adjustments and dividing responsibilities. Who will cook? Clean? Run errands? The first responder might adjust well to playing golf, fishing, or hanging out with other retirees, while the spouse can't get used to working hard knowing their significant other is having fun on their own or with friends or the kids.

The first responder might adjust well to playing golf, fishing, or hanging out with other retirees, while the spouse can't get used to working hard knowing their significant other is having fun on their own or with friends or the kids.

A difficult scenario would be if the spouse doesn't work or has already retired, and now the first responder retires and both are home together *all day*. I have to admit, that scenario still has the power to frighten me. Jeff home all day following me around? Even as a clinician helping others deal with the situation and a husband who understands the Work Brain/Home Brain split, I get nervous and fretful when I wonder, *How am I going to find my alone time?*

Both of you have to be patient and keep communicating. It took us first responder spouses a long time to adjust to the lifestyle. We can't adjust to a total about-face overnight. And if you need to retire early due to injury or ill health, there's even more to deal with. Perhaps you're faced with finding or training for another career. Or just figuring out what to do. If your family is losing income, you might feel panicky, especially if your children are still at home. And what's the first responder's go-to solution for feelings of doubt and panic? Pushing away the emotions and trying to just plow ahead, shutting down emotions and losing patience with your spouse if they show that they're worried, too. People who have always been in charge don't deal well with feeling helpless, and that alone is a solid reason to plan. A backup plan is mandatory. You never want to be trying to solve one crisis in the middle of another one. You always need to be prepared for an incident within an incident. Be aware of your rights and your medical coverage. Stay conscious of how your special skills as a first responder might translate to the outside world. Look both within and outside of fire, law enforcement, or EMS. And share your fears and feelings with your spouse.

Points to Think About:

1. The Work Brain/Home Brain split affects all first responders, and it doesn't end at retirement. Keep in mind that you and your spouse are facing a new life together, but that adjusting to the new normal isn't going to be a piece of cake. Both of you acknowledging this and talking things through will help because you *will* get on each other's nerves.

2. Being in fight-or-flight mode is part of the Work Brain scenario. It doesn't belong at home, especially when you're retired. Concentrate on not jumping at every little thing, being less critical, and talking things through. And never forget the change from barely there to constant togetherness puts as much strain on the rest of your family as it does on you.

3. The new normal won't arrive overnight. Don't give in to thinking everything is fine because you're hunting, fishing, or whatever else you've been longing to do and your significant other hasn't complained. Ask about what you don't understand, and don't just expect them to change their life just because of what you want to do. Open and honest channels of communication will help a lot and make your retirement a happy one.

CHAPTER SIX

When Those Old Calls Come Calling

Don't dismiss the power of your old calls coming back to haunt you just because you have never been diagnosed with PTSD. As soon as you're out of Work Brain for a long enough period, the brain automatically starts unpacking whatever old memories are stuffed away inside of it, like a suitcase stuffed with workout clothes forgotten in the attic. That's what gets first responders thrown for a loop after they retire and it hits them. Naturally, it's harder for those who have suffered from actual PTSD, but it affects almost *every* first responder who has had any disturbing calls that they tried to push out of their mind.

The natural reaction to this is to think, *What? Why now when I'm not even working anymore?* But that's exactly why it hits you when it does: because you're relaxing. It's almost as if Work Brain is determined not to let you forget the past and let Home Brain do its thing. If you have thirty years of calls that you haven't processed or talked about, they're going to start coming to the surface—not all of them, but certainly the ones that stood out in your memory but were shoved down: the dead kids, the suicides, the people burned alive in their beds.

I've found that a lot of crusty, old-school guys, the "Suck it up, Buttercup!" types who tend to shove everything down and ignore it, get freaked out when all those calls float back to the surface—ghosts they thought they had buried coming to haunt them. It scares them. If you know you have sought treatment for PTSD, then you have probably been taught that it never goes away and, with luck, you have also learned how to mitigate and decrease your symptoms, and how to be careful to avoid anything that triggers them. It is important to have some insight and be able to identify your triggers so you can plan accordingly. But don't make your triggers everyone else's responsibility. You must identify them and communicate them to your significant other and family, but it is up to you to implement healthy coping skills and seek professional help if triggers become unmanageable.

The ones who get the shock of their lives are those who retire thinking everything's cool and then in weeks, months, or years, the old calls come back. I will be discussing EMDR (Eye Movement Desensitization and Reprocessing) as an excellent technique for helping with trauma later in this chapter. Other interventions work, and EMDR isn't the only one, just one I prefer. As a clinician, I have relied upon it often when working with first responders who have suffered after traumatic events. One of these people was someone who had been with CHP for twenty-six years and had retired ten years before—and he was suddenly being tortured by calls he remembered from *the first year he was hired*. He kept asking me, "Why? Why now when I've been out for so long?"

It would be nice if when you sign your retirement papers, you could also hand the old calls in your head over to HR with your paperwork, but it doesn't work that way. Unresolved trauma will eventually physically manifest itself. There's an excellent book on the subject that I have recommended to quite a few first responders: *The Body Keeps the Score: Brain, Mind, and Body in the Healing of Trauma* by Bessel van der Kolk. We often forget that our brains are connected to our bodies and that one feeds off the other. Most people who have never been in therapy or seen a clinician don't think about the body's automatic responses.

It would be nice if when you sign your retirement papers, you could also hand the old calls in your head over to HR with your paperwork, but it doesn't work that way. Unresolved trauma will eventually physically manifest itself.

If you come from the older generation and just sucked it up, you may have convinced and tricked yourself into thinking that you have dealt with those calls and that the past can't hurt you. As a former first responder myself, I, too, came from the suck it up generation. It especially affected me as a female. I was even told by my partner, "Never let them see you cry." I have had to unpack my calls as you will, and while it's not easy, remember that you survived the actual event and this unpacking is just re-calling and processing it. I have met with retired first responders who are shocked and overwhelmed when it hits them and come to me asking, "What's wrong with me?"

If you have shoved down bad memories for decades, what do you expect your brain to do when you have finally relaxed enough and come off that adrenaline rush long enough for the awful visions to float back up to the surface of your mind? What did you think was going to happen?

What I do for a living now, helping first responders as a clinician, is fairly new. Cops have always had assistance available to deal with bad calls such as officer-involved shootings, but not to the degree they do now. And it's new to many other first responders. Peer support is much more prevalent now, so first responders have encouragement and empathetic debriefing from their peers to try to unpack the calls instead of pushing them down and holding onto them. But it's only in the last ten years that we've decided to talk about it.

It's generational. And this current generation is changing some of the old ideas and policies because they know those things don't work in the long term. But older generations grew up just thinking that pensions and getting good benefits would make them secure. The younger people have become comfortable sharing their entire lives—good, bad, or indifferent—all over social media, which makes them more open to the debriefing process.

So, what can you do when those old calls come a-callin'? It's extremely important to share your feelings with your spouse. Being in the job for years—often for more than half your life when you retire—can have a profound and unexpected effect on you. My husband was well aware of this already, especially after all the conversations we had when I was writing *Fully Involved*, and he says, "I think one of the biggest challenges is the loss of routine and *being*. We get recognized throughout our entire career for *being* something, and then it's gone. And we wonder, *What are we now?* For some first responders, it's been their entire purpose, all of it. And the stress of what we do, the fatigue, the tragedy, and then the criticism can grow and start affecting you differently. You become cynical. You can start to lose hope. You might start not to care. You feel like you're stuck on a carousel you can't get off."

You retire, relieved to be done with what you've spent a huge chunk of your life doing. Maybe you're bored. Maybe you're depressed. Maybe you feel your department betrayed you, let you down. Maybe you're pretty happy and enjoying the feeling of no more shifts, no more life-or-death situations to deal with, no more nerves tight as steel wires. I know that, as a clinician, I sometimes have a client talk about a call and that retelling triggers *me*. It's not the old 911 ambulance calls I struggle with; it's the more than twenty-five line-of-duty death (LODD) calls I have been through with fire and police. Doing debriefs means I have to hear over and over how someone died, with all the details. These memories have caused me more nightmares and distress than any call I've ever run myself. Even though I talk things over with my husband, I have also sought counseling to help me process them, but it's still something I struggle with, especially when I heard of an LODD. I also sometimes have anxiety just hearing about fires or something that happened involving police. I think dealing with this will always be a work in progress.

Like other first responders, Jeff has found dealing with old calls troublesome. "The old calls do weird things to me," he says. "It's almost as if I just finished the run. It's a superfast thought process."

Since no one tells first responders that once they slow down, all the traumatic calls they've shoved down and ignored will float to the surface, it's a shock to them when that happens. Some first responders have over thirty years of horrific images lodged in their heads, and most have done a good job of functioning despite these demons. But once the brain senses you're not in fight-or-flight mode anymore, it starts clearing out those calls. So, nightmares can increase, you can experience anxiety or get more easily irritated, and if you keep doing what you're used to doing—pushing it all back down—you'll fail to resolve something that just increases in strength.

Many people believe these issues will resolve themselves and go away after enough time passes. That may happen for some calls, but the ones that keep reoccurring, or that you're dreaming about or losing sleep over, are the ones telling you it's time to find outside help. Sometimes it's easier for those who *have* been diagnosed with PTSD in the past to recognize that the return of bad calls is something that can't just be pushed down forever. You need to process them. Most of all, you need to be prepared for them to hit you hard.

While Ethan didn't retire from being a paramedic due to PTSD but because of his back issues, he says he's had calls come back since being home all the time, even though he now feels more relaxed. Again, it's being more relaxed that allows the brain to start unpacking. There are several downsides to this, including recurring bad dreams, insomnia, and having the same old calls flashing back no matter how hard you try to ignore them.

"Calls from long ago come back," he says. "One kept waking me up in a cold sweat at two o'clock in the morning, around the time the call occurred. It was an auto accident with fire. People kept yelling at us to save the person behind the wheel, but because of the flames, we couldn't get close to it. We couldn't get the doors open, and they were trapped in there. All we could do was listen to the person suffering through that and then watch the car exploding. That call came back to me out of nowhere and kept me wide awake for two and a half hours."

Instead of ignoring those calls when they come back, Ethan deals with them. "I have to think them through," he says, "because trying to shove them back into Pandora's box just isn't going to happen right then and there. In the past, because I had the opportunity to teach scenarios in which I or someone else plays the victim, I would use those calls from my past, even the painfully thought-provoking and very hard ones or the ones not for the squeamish, because students have to learn how to deal with this themselves. By processing it, going over it as an educational process, I was able to deal with decades of bad calls.

"Then they took that outlet away from me, due to Covid-19 stopping in-class sessions during training. So, I had more problems once Covid started and I wasn't teaching. Not being able to teach during the pandemic meant that release wasn't there for me, so I had more problems with flashbacks during that period than ever before."

Bill was an undercover narcotics cop in one state and then with the sheriff's department in another for eight years until he quit to go into nursing. He has now been retired from law enforcement for more than ten years. He doesn't have old calls coming into his head, but he says, "Scenarios pop into my head. It hasn't been a frequent thing and, to be honest, the worst thing I ever dreamed about was when I had dreams of being in the jail. In my dreams, the bedroom was the control room, and the inmates were wandering around just outside of it. I remember waking up, grabbing my girlfriend, holding her down on the bed, and telling her to stay down because they were out there.

"There were times when I was working narcotics when sleeping next to me was not good. I'd get a simple twitch and start swinging. Now it's just dreams, and they're just stories—nothing violent the way they used to be."

The last time I spoke with Bill, I told him that I'm always telling my law enforcement clients that they ruined me because I can't sit with my back to the door anymore. I have to see the door, and I have to know where the other exit is. Honestly, I'm even more worried about that than my husband is. I wanted to know if Bill still had some of those tendencies. He said, "I have an awareness. I would say quite a strong awareness, but I try not to let it dictate what I do now so much because I see it more as a bit of paranoia. I can always tell you what people are wearing when they walk into a restaurant or other place and then where they're sitting. I am just aware of everybody around me."

Sometimes, taking positive steps away from the things that trigger those bad calls coming back is the answer. Jim, the fire-fighter who retired due to PTSD and had trouble with bad calls hitting him when he took a part-time job delivering pizzas, says that when he and Mary moved to a different state, he was no longer nearly as troubled or anxious. He had left behind all the sites that brought him flashbacks. He says that some of his close friends back at the department have started reevaluating calls they pushed down. "They know that I went through it and that I'm getting better, but that I still have it. It's not like it just goes away. And some of them say, 'Gosh, I have a lot of unresolved things, too.' I tell them, 'You should go talk to a counselor or

even to a trauma retreat.' After all, the department pays for it."
Not all departments will cover it, but there are some retreats
that are meant for first responders or military only.

Eye Movement Desensitization and Reprogramming

While various approaches are used to treat PTSD and other psychological conditions in which you can't control your thoughts or reaction, I want to tell you about EMDR, the therapy I consider a wise choice for trauma resolution. I have worked using EMDR on all types of first responders to relive and relieve trauma from disturbing, tragic, and/or painful incidents. So, in case any of your worst calls come back, I want you to have the proper information close at hand.

EMDR is an evidence-based psychotherapy treatment created in the late 1980s to alleviate the distress caused by disturbing memories. It's been successful in relieving the distress triggered by those memories, with as high as 80 percent success in treating PTSD. EMDR helps people reformulate their negative beliefs and gain a more positive outlook, as well as reducing both physical and emotional distress. I have had great results using my EMDR training to help first responders with those bad calls, flashbacks, and PTSD.

EMDR works on our brain's information-processing system. We all have one of these. It's how we store memories, through network links in the brain that hold related thoughts, sensations, emotions, and images. Our information systems aren't perfect, and the process can remain incomplete when something happens—or even when we hear about something—that's traumatic.

Our information systems aren't perfect, and the process can remain incomplete when something happens—or even when we hear about something— that's traumatic.

We still store the memory, but it goes into one of the other networks that lack the appropriate connections that should be associated with it. So, when that memory is triggered, it sets off strong emotions and physical reactions. This can happen even if the trauma wasn't a major one.

EMDR works to separate extreme reactions from triggering events. Sessions are usually one or two times per week for six to twelve sessions with a trained clinician, though often fewer sessions are required. Focusing directly on the memory, treatment can change the way the memory is stored in your brain, reducing and even eradicating the symptoms. EMDR is based on the theory that recalling traumatic events becomes less upsetting when your attention is diverted. So, in short bouts, you relive the event or the triggering of the flashback while your clinician directs your eye movements. After just a single session, many people feel calmer and better able to cope. EMDR has been found to work for anxiety, panic, traumatic incidents, and full-blown PTSD. Several of the first responders you have heard from in this book have found relief through the desensitization process.

Points to Think About:

1. You don't need to have been diagnosed with PTSD to experience triggering and bad calls coming back to unsettle you. And many lifers don't even know if they ever had PTSD because it wasn't a frequent diagnosis back when they started working.

2. Bad calls can be triggered by a sound, image, or even a smell that suddenly connects to a memory you have pushed down that comes back to haunt you now that you're retired and your brain is unpacking everything you didn't deal with at the time. They can be the cause of nightmares, insomnia, anxiety, and depression.

3. Bad calls do tend to come back. You pushed them away at the time. But now is the time to get help if they interfere with your life. EMDR is one of the most dependable and successful treatments because it makes new connections in your memory processing so that when the memory comes to you, it is no longer so distressing. You can learn more about EMDR or how to find an EMDR practitioner in your state here: https://www.emdria.com.

CHAPTER SEVEN

Hobbies Aren't Just for Kids

What will you be doing on, if not a daily schedule, at least regularly once you're retired? How will you fill your time? Do you have hobbies that you already pursue? And why do you need to start planning right now? I want to share some ideas with you so you won't find yourself sitting staring at the television or into space once you've gotten over the luxury of sleeping late and doing whatever you feel like doing whenever you want to do it.

My survey results showed that 89 percent of the first responders felt positive about hobbies and future pastimes but weren't going too far afield from the things they've been doing, not thinking about new things to try. Over a quarter of them (25.93 percent) wanted to spend more time camping and fishing, while 51.83 percent were big on other outdoor activities and 22.22 percent are evenly divided between those who golf and those who like swimming and water sports.

Some of the other things retirees who don't plan on starting new full-time careers are looking to do are getting part-time jobs or working as a volunteer, catching up on reading books, working out, becoming a trainer, coaching children's sports, and traveling. But if that's all you can come up with in terms of hobbies, I'm here to remind you that most of us spend a minimum of sixteen hours a day wide awake. That time is yours to fill.

Why do you need to fill that time? So you and your spouse don't drive each other up the wall! Seriously, if Jeff had decided to fully retire and not take another job, while it would be a blessing in some areas, such as having days in the week free to do things or go out on a date because we'd both be off all day, we would have had to find ways to do things on our own. I'm sure most of you agree with me that 24/7 togetherness is not a necessity after the honeymoon. but it's easy to fall into even if it isn't fun. Getting some hobbies now is a way to start establishing your new normal not-joined-at-the-hip before your retirement. Keep in mind that your spouse or significant other has spent a career learning to not have you around all the time, make decisions without you, or even just having alone time. Don't take it personally if they get annoyed at the idea of you being home all the time. It will be an adjustment for them too. It will make the time spent together more enjoyable.

First responders and those they've settled down with tend to be resilient anyhow, but that resiliency can fade quickly when faced with a very different life than what they were expecting or are used to. You need to be both resilient and flexible. For instance, since Jeff and I now have to do all our "together" things pretty much on the weekends, I have started taking Wednesdays off. One reason is that I'm fully booked, and seeing clients five days a week would burn me out. But in addition to needing an extra break, I wanted to have a "me" day, the type of day I was used to having for up to six days at a time. I enjoy having Wednesdays to myself. I clean the house and run errands. Some days I run, while some I spend at the gym, I can eat whatever I want for dinner even if it's a bowl of cereal, I get to watch whatever I want on TV, and the best part is I can have the thermostat at whatever temp I want. I just do my own thing.

Many couples, like Jim and Mary, had planned to fully retire but decided to take part-time jobs to have a purpose that included somewhere to go and something to do. Both work for

FedEx and are satisfied with their choice and happy to have the extra income. I have found that those who are happiest with full retirement often still have children at home and are grateful for the opportunity to help raise them and be able to enjoy all the things they missed out on in the past. Some are grandparents and wholeheartedly enjoy that role—though it's important to know when and where to draw the line. I have a friend who's become practically a full-time babysitter since his retirement and who tells me he works harder than ever before. Sometimes he enjoys it but not always.

You need to be flexible while at the same time setting boundaries. Boundaries are the key. For instance, another friend's wife, after he retired, was exhausted by his texting her constantly. But just because you're both retired doesn't mean you need to be in each other's space the entire time. But also realize that this huge change can cause anxiety and uncertainty for both. You are creating a whole new normal and routine. If you stop what you're doing to answer someone's every call or text, you need to do this. You can do it nicely. Just say, "These are the things I'll be doing. Please don't call or text unless it's an emergency and I'll be in touch as soon as I finish." If you say nothing, you have no grounds for complaint. You can't expect people to read your mind and know what you like or don't like. And it isn't the same for everyone. I know that if and when I become a grandmother, I will probably cut my hours significantly because I want my grandchildren to be babysat by me rather than strangers.

Open Your Mind to Possibilities

In keeping with the saying about first responders constantly craving new stimuli yet hating change, you might find it challenging to even want to *try* something new. The first requirement here if you don't want to be miserable in retirement is to be willing to get out of your comfort zone. There's no magic answer: this journey of retirement means embracing the hard stuff, which is not going to be comfortable. If you won't get outside of your comfort zone, what are you going to do in the years ahead, how will you ever do anything? You're just going to sit there wondering what happened when you've dreamed for so long of being able to retire.

It is a mindset. It's literally what you tell yourself. Let's say growing tomatoes is something you've always wanted to do but you can't get motivated. What have you been telling yourself? That it will take too much time or effort? That it's not going to work? That you're not going to be good at it? What we tell ourselves affects us and whether we embrace or dismiss an idea. I practice a lot of cognitive-behavioral therapy with clients because if you're negative and think you can't do something, you can't.

It's important not to get locked into the final big picture where you see yourself only as either having a flourishing vegetable garden or just a few scraggly plants or managing to achieve full fluency in a language on the one hand versus being an embarrassing failure on the other. You need to take small bites, starting small and growing gradually. And you need to set goals.

The most helpful thing here is that you write it down. When we have ideas or thoughts in our head they are abstract and can sound very different when you speak them. But writing it down activates a different sense and makes it more concrete. This way too you can mark off the goals as you achieve them and see how far you have come.

Setting short-term goals for anything new will help you keep going. Say you want to learn to speak French or Spanish. Sure, it might be fun to go to France or Spain right away, but that's not practical for most people. You need to take a small step in the beginning. That could mean looking for an inexpensive in-person group class through a local university's adult study program or taking an online course. You don't even need to spend money if you check websites like YouTube for freebies or look online for free introductory courses.

Make your mantra, "Now I get to explore this hobby or training I've always thought about doing" and not "Now I have to do this." No, it's I "get" to do this.

I always wanted to learn to scuba dive, and when Jeff and I went on vacation to a resort that offered free beginner's classes, I did my best to cajole him into our doing it together. He just wasn't into it, though, so I didn't. But it stuck in my brain, and I ended up doing it later with our son. Kyle and I both loved it, and it became a mother-son bonding experience. So, do try something whether it's ice-skating lessons, skydiving in an assisted jump, or signing up for a cooking class. Jeff and Megan have just started taking a cooking class, and he loves it. Mainly, he loves that he gets to do things with the kids that he didn't get to when they were younger. He's kind of getting a redo. Don't pooh-pooh something or minimize what you think you'd love. Don't worry if anyone else thinks it's a silly idea. You're not at the station or firehouse anymore. There's no peer pressure now. Just give yourself permission and do it, and if you don't like it, guess what? You can quit. It's that easy.

You don't just need hobbies, of course. You also need a schedule. Why? Because you've lived a large part of your life on one. When you're used to having regimentation in your life, being free as a bird isn't always a blessing. You will miss having to be someplace and do something on a charted schedule—in other words, you can feel lost without the things you always moaned about. Well, you're going to be your own drill instructor from now on.

Having a schedule doesn't mean it needs to be strict, but in our lifestyle, we've always known what we're going to do on this date or that. Having a schedule from the start will help you transition into retirement. We now have blackout curtains in the bedroom so we sleep well (and, equally important to me, so I can keep sleeping when Jeff gets up around six or six-thirty).

He lets the dogs out, makes his coffee, and watches the news. Then, when he comes back to take a shower and dress to get to work at eight, I get up. I start work later so there's no need for me to rise earlier, and Jeff likes his "alone time" just as I like mine. We schedule in date nights, including one per month to go out and see a show, an idea Jeff came up with that's perfect for Las Vegas.

You can schedule most of your activities, whether it's going kayaking every week, trail-running most days, taking a class, or shopping days. If you work full-time, part-time, or freelance, that all goes on your schedule as well. If travel is your interest, you can slot that in as well. If you don't plan to work, you can volunteer with a charity or do something for your church or any clubs you join. It is a well-known fact that volunteering can decrease depression. Soon you'll have a calendar filled with dates. It will keep you in the groove of feeling useful, knowing you have events and meetings you look forward to.

You can start opening your mind right now, even if you're not retiring for several years. And once you have retired, if you're open to trying new things, you might find you love things you never even dreamed about. Steve, who moved to Utah, now enjoys assisting his significant other's family with farming. "I live in a farming ranch town, so I lend a hand with branding cattle, mending fences, and other farm chores," he says. "I never thought I'd be doing these things, but I enjoy it."

Wesley, who also moved to Utah, volunteers with the local sheriff's department. "I go out and help fill the gaps in patrolling different areas where deputies can't do it because these guys here are seriously spread out. I can help out four or five hours a week."

When I speak with retired friends and clients, I can sometimes hear the difference between those who have schedules and those who are still just free-floating into retirement. Feeling useful and knowing you have someplace to go and something to do makes all the difference. Whether you choose to have a career, work part-time, or fully retire, a schedule will provide you with a sense of purpose. Plus, having things to do and people to see will help you make new friends and get over not seeing the old ones regularly, which—in most cases—you won't.

Old Friends, New Friends

You *will* drift apart from friends who were like family. They *were* your family, your other one, the one you spent almost as much time with as your significant other, spouse, or kids. "You do lose touch with many of them," Jeff says of how much he sees or hears from his old work family in retirement. "It's a fact of life, and you need to face it. They move or you move; you develop other interests. They go on with their lives, which aren't about your old workplace anymore. That's over. There's a new life happening now for you and others who retire, and it doesn't revolve around the job. There are still many connections, but it's not as much a part of your routine. And some friendships with that former second family will just fade away completely, especially if you or they move to another state."

Think back to when you were in high school. You and your classmates spent four years being together all day. When you graduated, you promised you'd stay in touch, but life happens, and we grow apart. It's the same with first responders. You are literally scheduled to be with each other, forced to get close and bond. But when you retire, staying close requires an effort and time carved out of every person's day. Friends who haven't yet retired will find that difficult to fit it, just as you did when your time was limited by working and you wanted to spend time off with your family—the people you loved and never got to be with enough. So, you need to not take it personally when friends drift away; you can't make it personal or feel you didn't matter or have been cast aside.

As far as keeping friends goes, some of it depends on how much time you spent with your work family on days when you weren't working. Steve says, "If you have this vast circle of friends from your department that you were always in touch with, it's different. How some coworkers enter retirement can be vastly different from how it is for you.

"I wouldn't recommend anybody single move out of state when they retire," he cautions. "I cried myself to sleep many times because I felt so alone. I didn't have a relationship; I didn't know anybody. I met some neighbors and other good people, but I was completely lost. In the first six months after I'd moved, I went back to California a couple of times—and I spent a lot of time asking myself, *What did you just do?*"

Luckily, he met the woman he now lives with and stopped wondering, *What do I have? What if I really need someone? Who's my go-to person?* And because she's a local and has a large family, Steve's circle of acquaintances expanded greatly. Still, he says, "I'm in my tenth year of retirement and I still struggle. Your life just transitions so much. You don't realize while it's happening, while you're in it, how much you identify with your first responder career and friends."

Making new friends is a goal worth putting effort into. Part-time jobs can help. And you won't necessarily lose touch with everyone. Ethan still has buddies from his EMT days. "Some will be friends for life," he says. "Our old dispatchers are still on my Facebook feed. Many have moved on with their careers and their lives; some have retired. One friend I've kept is inherently poor at keeping in touch, but when he does and we get together, we start talking as if we'd seen each other the week before. The bond is still there." And because Ethan continues to teach, he has retained that connection to his former career.

You can and will make new friends, but you have to be open to it as well as figuring out what type of people you'd like to hang out with. When you're with people all day at work, making friends is easy and convenient. Don't give up if you and someone new you thought might be a great friend simply don't gel. You need to try out new friends just as you try out new clothes. Some may fit and some you may need to return. You may have to look actively for opportunities to meet people, especially if you won't be working at all. Many of the first responders I interviewed for this book already had made friends through their church or volunteering. Not long after they moved, Ethan and Lori were pleased when they were invited to spend New Year's Eve at the home of people they'd met at church.

Church and local branches of organizations such as the Elks or Chamber of Commerce can be a good way to meet people. Jim and Mary, both of whom work part-time at FedEx, say they've made most of their new friends at work, though they've also become friends with people met through their church. And while Jim's favorite pastimes in retirement are fishing and golfing, Mary keeps busy and has made friends volunteering more at church.

Wesley, after leaving law enforcement and settling in Utah, not only started doing his volunteer work with the sheriff's department—he and his wife quickly joined a church which asked him to revamp the church's security team, which is now equipped with radios and specific assignments every Sunday. "We recently finished hosting a small group at our home for eight weeks of watching a course called Biblical Citizenship," he says, "and I've taught some six-week Constitution courses." With his own work as a travel representative and a home office, he's so satisfied with his life now he hadn't even taken advantage of many opportunities to travel.

When you're looking to make friends, you need to keep in mind that civilians are a different breed or you're the different breed. They haven't spent a lot of time looking at dead bodies, making arrests, dealing with distraught people and 911 calls or running into burning buildings. They usually don't share first responders' dark sense of humor or matter-of-fact way of talking about death, disaster, and bloodshed. That means regular folks aren't prepared for it. Sometimes you need to sit back and listen well to get a grasp of how other people talk in social groups. You want to learn what's fitting and what isn't if you don't want to shock or risk distressing someone you'd like to get to know better.

The main thing is that, as with hobbies, you have to be open to getting outside your comfort zone; making friends means asking questions and showing interest in what people have to say even though you're used to giving orders or being the leader. And you must never forget that many of the things we in the first responder world consider perfectly acceptable topics of conversation or ways to put things could be no-go areas to regular citizens. When conversing with new friends, it's always wise to follow their lead.

Why Work? Why Not?

It's a reassuring daydream when you're working hard in First Responder World: you see yourself sitting back, in a lawn chair, recliner, or poolside chaise lounge, doing nothing. Or maybe you imagine yourself sitting on a pier at your favorite fishing spot, enjoying the peace and quiet as you wait for a bite. And you're thinking, *Man, that's the life! I'm never going to work again.* But the reality is often different.

So, why work? In terms of choosing a whole new career, it's often because you're too young. Maybe you retired super early due to PTSD, an injury, or illness. Maybe you didn't put enough cash into your savings for retirement to be what you'd envisioned. Perhaps you have kids to raise or support. Maybe there's something you have always longed to do and you see this as your chance to build a flourishing second career. Regardless of why, there's when—and when should be before you retire for one big reason: what you decide to do in the future could have a bearing on whether or not you move or stay put so you want to make this part of your long-term planning as much as you can, depending on the situation. Obviously we can't plan for everything before we retire but that being said thinking about it and talking about it with your significant other at least starts the dialogue and thought process. Jeff and I had never planned to move to Nevada. We knew we wanted to leave California but were thinking of different places. If we weren't open-minded about all the possibilities we may have not even discussed moving here. No plan is perfect or goes off without a hitch. My main message here is not to just dream about what your retirement will look like but put some of those thoughts into action prior to the big day. I can't tell you how many people have said to me, "I could retire today and be happy." Maybe but more times than not it won't be as you expect it to be.

I'll look at all the factors that might influence any decision to stay or move in the next chapter. Right now, let's just give some thought to the benefits and drawbacks of working full-time.

Here are possible benefits of a new career:

- It will feed your thirst for a challenge.
- It will allow you to afford to do more and live better when you take that second retirement.
- If you retired from an injury, illness, or PTSD, it could make you feel healthier and feed your self-esteem as an actively contributing member of the community.
- It will open you to learning new things, make it easier to meet people, and bring you new experiences.
- Keeping your brain active has been proved to extend your life, memory, and cognitive abilities as you age.

There can also be drawbacks, such as:

- If you have children—whether at home or living nearby—that you looked forward to spending more time with, a new job might make that difficult or impossible.

- You will have to pre-plan vacations and have limits on vacation days.
- You will have to adapt to a set schedule and stick to it.
- You won't necessarily be looked upon as a leader, and you might have to start at entry-level and work your way up.
- The positions available to you might leave you cold.
- It may be hard to adjust to a civilian job.

Jeff was lucky. He was speaking with public utilities about working for them, but nothing felt right. He even got a few offers but after we talked about it, it just wasn't what he wanted. Then he lucked out with the job at UNLV, something that relies on his talents and know-how but is also fresh and challenging. As I've said, this did not affect our decision to move—we moved before Jeff got hired, when he was still considering utilities. Instead, it was almost magical how he found a position that he couldn't have designed better himself.

What if you want a new career but want to have more flexibility timewise? You can always start your own business to put your hard-earned first responder skills to use or, like Wesley starting a travel agency, get something out of it that appeals to you (in his case, he liked the idea of reduced prices for travel and the freedom to work from home).

Joe, who retired from the fire department due to cancer, started at twelve dollars an hour with the company he used when doing the purchasing at work. He's now the vice president. Bill, the former undercover narcotics officer, became as a nursing assistant as soon as he quit the force, while getting his bachelor's and RN degrees. Josh, who retired due to stress in 2020, is now a drug and alcohol counselor. He had been part owner of a detox center for drugs and alcohol in the past and chose to go back to that because, as he says, "It's good to be able to interact with the clients, and I find it spiritually fulfilling for me seeing guys come in feeling desperate and then seeing that light come on and watching them make it. I'm totally committed to my work."

If you don't want a new career, if you think you'd be happy doing several things, working online like teaching or taking on a part-time job or two, you can live anywhere. No matter where you go, you can build your new normal, make friends, and find plenty to do—as long as you stay open and optimistic about the future and view retirement as the exciting adventure it will be for you!

Points to Think About:

1. Have a schedule and stick to it. You'll want to block time for your existing hobbies and as well as new endeavors you'd like to try, date nights, family time, workouts, and everything else you can pre-plan, including your "me time."

2. Be open and willing to get out of your comfort zone. Whether to meet people and make new friends or to find new hobbies, getting out there in the world will enrich your life and fill your time constructively.

3. Try to keep all the pluses in your mind if you feel lonely or depressed at no longer having your work family. You now can spend more time with your own family or, if you're single, more opportunities to meet a future significant other. If you plan to work full-time, you can start thinking right now about what you might like to do: where you can use your skills and what you would enjoy. You can make your dreams come true, but those dreams aren't going to come knocking at your door. You need to put yourself out there as hard as you did when you applied to your current position as a first responder.

PART THREE

What to Do Now, Then, and Later

W e're getting down to the nitty-gritty now, the final details you need to think about and deal with before you retire as a first responder. You will face areas requiring planning regardless of how soon you retire or whether you plan on any type of employment or not. The details are every bit as important as how you'll fill your days. In fact, many of them will directly influence what you do in retirement.

Where will you live? Will you stay where you are or move? Downsize or buy a bigger place? Divide your time between two places or maybe buy an RV or a boat? If you move, will it be nearby or to another state? Will you rent or buy? And how do you begin to do all these things? What can be done in advance?

And what about the financial details? What could you start doing right away? What will you need to live on comfortably in retirement? Not surprisingly, most first responders told me they wished they had saved more in the past. You can begin now.

And, finally, you need to look at your relationship with your significant other or spouse. Do you have unresolved issues? Do you look forward to spending the rest of your lives together? As the saying goes, the devil is in the details. And I want to help you make sure no nasty imp is waiting there to catch you out just when you think you're going to be able to kick back and enjoy the good life!

CHAPTER EIGHT

Should You Stay or Should You Go?

You may not have given any thought to where you'll live once you retire, especially if that day lies far ahead. But it's important to have an idea of the possibilities and what appeals to you so you can keep that in mind when making plans because what you think you'd like to do can mean making choices sooner rather than later.

For instance, if you choose to stay in your house because it's almost or already paid off, you might want to fix it up or upgrade some things. Perhaps you'd like to put some money into a time-share or vacation home. Some people, like Ethan and Lori, decided to sell their home, buy an RV and travel for a few years, then look for a new house wherever they decide to settle.

Many first responders choose not to stick with what they've got. If you think you'd like to move out of the state you're in but aren't sure what state or states might suit you best, it's not a bad idea to start planning vacations around the spots you think you'd like. Look at travel articles and real estate sites; keep a file on possible places to live. Consider some of the possibilities that might tempt you elsewhere: a lower cost of living, no state taxes (an expert will be giving you advice on this in the next chapter), friends or family who live in another area, more of the activities you like, perhaps more like-minded people.

We're all attracted to different opportunities: those with families might be most motivated by a choice of good school districts with a high percentage of high school graduates going on to college while those who are retiring young but don't have families might want to be closer to big cities or resort areas that offer more in the way of diversion. If you put water sports on your list of future activities, you might choose to be closer to a river, ocean, or lake. Make a list of what you envision existing in or close to the ideal spot for your retirement, separating what you would like to find there that's less important from what you absolutely need. Then, fill out the list, adding anything you consider attractive—maybe activities for your kids or resources you might need if you have a child with special needs or an elderly parent living with you; maybe certain nearby medical facilities or specialists if you or your spouse has a health condition that requires recurring treatment. This will not only help you find the right areas but will also help you clarify exactly what you want and need.

Once you have an idea of areas in your state or different states where you might like to live, do more intensive research, not forgetting to look at the laws regarding pensions for the states that interest you. Jeff and I knew we would leave California once he was retired, and we had narrowed it down to several states before deciding on one not even on the list: Nevada. Why Las Vegas? It offered a great combination for us: lower cost of living; a never-ending choice of entertainment, sports, and the great outdoors; a good business environment; and the prime factor of being closer to our daughter and son-in-law. It wasn't on our list, but our son deciding to move to Las Vegas sealed the deal for us. And we're still thrilled to have both us and the kids in the same spot now. Jeff had always told me the desert wasn't really his thing, but as the saying goes, "Happy wife, happy life." And once we did our research, he was all for it. And I can tell you now that when I ask if he's happy in Vegas he tells me, "More than I ever thought possible." (See? I'm always right.)

Once you've decided on one place or are down to two or three, you can start adding the particulars in terms of what you're looking for in a neighborhood and housing. Again, ask yourself what would fit in with your vision of retirement. And be sure to discuss everything with your spouse or significant other and not rush into any decisions. Does the area have good schools and solid curriculums for children the age of yours? How do utility prices differ from where you are now or the other places on your list? Does the area offer opportunities for any sports you plan to pursue: running tracks, hiking or biking trails, golf courses, beaches or public pools, and affordable fitness centers? Are there enough entertainment facilities, sports venues, and varied religious institutions as well as a wide choice of supermarkets, big-box stores, and restaurants? If you're thinking of starting your own business, would you find the type of clients you want? If you're looking for a full-time career, does the local economy appear to be in good shape?

If you're currently living somewhere where everything is accessible, you might be faced with choices that never occurred to you and that will mean compromising. If you dream of traveling to faraway places, not being in proximity to an airport can be a dealbreaker. The pleasures of travel—even if it's just to visit family members on one coast when you'd prefer to live on the other—can wear thin when preceded by a three-hour drive to and from the closest airport. Travel isn't cheap, either, so you might prefer to spend that part of your budget seeing the world or the rest of the country rather than just visiting family. We all have our quirks and what we want to have on hand. Some people don't want to live far from a Costco or a specific supermarket chain; some want to be able to go to a favorite football team's home stadium. Knowing what you want is the first step in finding the right place.

What Will You Need? What Will You Want?

It isn't only a choice between staying where you are or moving to a new area. You also need to think about whether or not you want to change in terms of housing. It used to be that anyone who switched houses to retire traded down to something smaller. That's no longer true. Let's say you currently live under an hour's drive from your grown children but want to move someplace that requires five hours or more in a car. Chances are your kids and grandchildren won't just be dropping in but will be coming to stay for at least several days at a time. In that case, or if you're moving to an area you expect more friends will want to visit, you might be looking for more space. If you plan to stay put but wonder how much you could lower your overhead or sell and trade down to a condo or a rental, you need to do some research. Whether you scale up or down is a personal choice but an important one to think about and one that you and your significant other need to discuss in depth before you start looking.

You need to consider many possibilities when you move *anywhere*, local or long-distance, for the simple reason that you aren't just going to move out of your current home into a new one but out of the entire lifestyle you've followed for many years. Will your extended family be growing? Do you have much more space than you need? If you own your home, is it (or will it probably be) a good time to make a profit by trading down? Do you want to take a year off and travel around the country, living in your RV, making your hunt for a new place to live an adventure? Do you want to escape from winter weather or get away from a state where the summers have turned too sizzling for you?

Moving out of state is a huge venture, and I think it's impossible to prepare for everything. But learning more about wherever you're planning to relocate will help you when you get there. The transition isn't just a cultural or emotional change—a lot of tasks come with it, and the more you know in advance, the better equipped you will be. We had to research all sorts of things, including getting new healthcare insurance, the cost of car insurance in a different state, and finding new doctors and dentists. Use your network if you know others who moved to different states or consider pooling your information with others. Know someone who moved out of the state you're in now and loves it? You might ask if they're willing to be your guide if you go check things out.

Until moving, I had never thought much about how rooted we get in our communities. It has nothing to do with how much we get out. The comfort of knowing where everything is and how to get what you need can't be underrated. Nor can climate, even if you don't move far, far away. You'll need to adapt. Even though Southern California gets as hot as Las Vegas in the summer, we weren't prepared for the dryness. Buying a large humidifier solved that, but the year-round dryness (with, of course, flash floods that do little to increase the humidity for long) was a surprise even after having spent time here through the years. It's like people who move from Illinois or Ohio to Virginia or Tennessee and think they won't need their heavy clothes anymore. Even the people where you're going can be different; there can be a whole different vibe from state to state. I couldn't get over the difference in driving habits. Nevada is chill compared to aggressive California driving. I had to tell myself to slow down, that the traffic isn't filled with the gridlocks I was used to so I can relax. Each state has its own culture and way of doing things, and it might take you some time to get used to that as well as the weather.

Maybe you don't want to rush into relocating. When I last spoke with Ethan and Lori, they planned to start their RV travel in 2022, checking out the Boise, Idaho, and Prescott, Arizona, areas as well as hitting Alaska and Canada. They don't know where they might end up, but they're looking forward to the adventure.

Or you might be like Bill. He was living in Sarasota working with the sheriff's department there when he made the transition from patrol to narcotics, then he worked narcotics in Michigan for fifteen years. When he retired and decided to go into nursing, he went back to Sarasota. "There was a fifteen-year gap," he says. "But it's like I never left. I'm still friends with the same people and in touch with some of my old neighbors. I'm back to hanging out with guys I used to work with." You *can* go home again when you retire. You can go pretty much wherever you want.

Jeff and I knew we would relocate to a smaller place since it's just us two now. And because we don't want to move again as we get older, we had agreed on a single-story home. I wanted a new place that was ours alone because I never liked dealing with other people's poor upkeep or oddball decorating decisions. Having lived in the same house for eighteen years, I was excited about a new build where we could choose what we wanted in terms of flooring, fixtures, and paint colors. A local friend recommended a real estate agent, and we found our new house during a three-day visit. Even better, the agent had a fully furnished house she rents out, so it was easy to pack and store our things until our home was ready.

Because we had already created our list of necessities and desires, finding the right part of town and the best location within it for our new life didn't take much time. The area is rapidly expanding, with people moving in from all over the country, so there are houses and apartment complexes going up in any direction. We were able to move into our newly finished home just five months after we'd sold our house in California. We're happy there, including the dogs, and it's close enough to our children that we can see them often. We have already created some rituals of Sunday football, my daughter and I working out, and Jeff and Megan cooking together.

I think when you find the right place, it just hits you because it feels like this is where you could be comfortable and happy. Wesley told me that after deciding against some states on their list for various reasons, he and his wife settled on the wide, open spaces of Utah but weren't sure what kind of residence they needed. When they started to look, they were shown a piece of land that felt perfect. "The realtor said, 'Hey, for five hundred bucks, you can put a hold on this property,' and that did it," Wesley told me. "My wife pulled out her checkbook and that was the moment when everything became real." You, too, will have your own stepping-off point if you decide to make a move.

In the beginning, it was disorienting, moving first to a rental and then to our new place in what was just the fourth move in our twenty-six years of marriage. We all get stuck in our ways, and we also get stuck in our old neighborhoods. You need to accept that you'll be facing all sorts of new things, including that you're going to be disoriented in a place. Be prepared to get lost and don't tell yourself that using GPS is for babies. I would think I knew perfectly well how to get to our new local hardware supply after having been there once or twice—until I found myself cruising along a busy street wondering, *Where the heck am I?*

I went from having been able to drive almost anywhere I wanted in Southern California without maps or apps to relying on GPS to tell me how to get to the grocery store or the post office. You get seasoned pretty quickly when you move, even more so if you move someplace that's spread out; you'll still end up wondering where you've gotten to at times whereas a couple of months earlier you knew every stoplight and street corner in your area. Don't worry. Everything will eventually become routine, just as it was before. And remember the pluses of leaving the area where you worked: you will no longer drive past the scene of a fatal car crash or the house where you did CPR on a child.

Leaving Your Old Life

Moving in also requires moving out. That means giving advance notice if you've been renting or listing your house if you're selling. Real estate markets go hot and cold, but preparations for giving up a property remain. You may be excited to be leaving or a bit sad, but you will surely have your hands full getting out of where you are before you can get into your new life. Jeff and I had moments where we both were wondering if we had bitten off more than we could chew or screwed up in decision-making. Leaving an old life behind is a loss and you have to allow yourself some grace and space for grieving.

If you're renting, you will save money by making sure nails are out of walls, minor repairs get done, and the home is spotless before you have management come in for inspection. You'll pay a lot more if they decide anything doesn't count as "normal wear and tear" and charge you plenty to fix it. If you're selling, you want to be able to list your house as "turnkey" or "move-in ready." I was surprised by what it takes to optimize a home for a fast sale. You may not be a designer, but you still have to "stage" the house to look its best and reflect neutrality and not your personal preferences. Make a plan and do one project at a time.

If you want your own move-in to be flawless, you might want to have area rugs or upholstered furniture cleaned professionally before moving out. Or like us, you might purge and hold some garage or yard sales. And you can enjoy some old memories as you do so. Or you might prefer to wait since most moving companies have small-print clauses about what they consider their responsibilities and will often fight to the death if you want them to cover any damage they caused, even though you've paid for insurance. Next, you need to decide if you would prefer that they pack for you. This can also cost more than you've bargained for, as packers use about twice as much wrapping and packing material than you might and you get billed for that as well as the hourly rate for packing. On the other hand, your paying them to pack everything up might be a necessity if you want any expensive items covered by insurance. Or, like us, you might pack and move yourself with pods, hiring movers to pack the pods on one end and unpack on the other. Figuring out what will work best for you is part of the process. Does this all sound like too much? Jeff has a friend who retired at end of 2021, and he and his wife were going to live in a rented apartment in France. I envied them their adventure, and something similar might be a welcome break from all the moving stress.

One good reason to clear out is that you will pay a price for everything that gets moved. This is a good thing, and you'll also get a tax write-off for charitable donations or a bit of pocket money for consignment or other resale options. This is especially important if you're moving from a house into an apartment or just downsizing in general. You never miss an extra closet until you don't have one. And you don't want to be one of those people who pays for self-storage year after year—long after forgetting what's even being stored—do you? Decide what's replaceable and what isn't before you end up getting rid of stuff *after* you've paid to move it.

Most moving companies, and even the US Postal Service, offer free checklists of things to do before moving. The lists are self-evident but valuable, even if just to remind yourself when to close your current bank account or cancel your current home insurance policy. You can also find these checklists easily online and there will almost certainly be a few items there you might have overlooked.

Whether you plan to rent or buy, you can always get an idea of what's available in your chosen destination. Most real estate sites also supply other information, such as homeowner association fees and what it covers as well as the sales history of any property; rental listings usually come with a full breakdown of amenities. The most important thing of all? Don't let moving get you down. Sadness at what you're leaving behind will be mitigated by your excitement at starting a new life in a new place that you will soon make your own.

Points to Think About:

1. Your way of life is going to change, which gives you a chance to make changes that can make your life easier and more pleasurable. Exploring new possibilities is one of those changes, and you can start by deciding if you want to stay put or move, leave the state or just the house you're in. It's not a chore but an opportunity to find and learn about places that could help bring you a joyful retirement.

2. Even if you're not leaving town, you might want to leave your current residence for something larger or smaller. It's never too early to start thinking about what would best suit you. If you think it's time to trade up or down, you can decide what type of residence would suit your needs and wants, then get an idea of costs in the areas that appeal to you. Even if this doesn't seem like a big issue now because you're young, it can affect you when you're ready to retire. Don't let your age give you a false sense of security: be mindful and remember that the long-term costs are important.

3. Both moving out and moving in require planning and forethought. Much of this can't be accomplished far in advance, but once you're pretty sure you'd like to move, you can start gathering information about moving options and requirements. And it's always a good time to get rid of items you no longer need rather than ending up paying to move excess baggage.

CHAPTER NINE

The Practical Stuff

By this point, I think you realize how important being prepared is. I want you to have as much information as possible on what to do and how to do it, so you don't end up less comfortable in your new life than you would have if you had taken care of more things farther in advance of retiring (unless it's a forced retirement, of course, and then having prepared in advance will be life-changing in every way. And, trust me, if you don't have a fully developed plan, you will risk ending up shocked and disappointed just like:

- the 38.10 percent who don't envision their lives changing greatly in retirement.
- the 92.75 percent who say they would have been helped by getting more education on retirement throughout their careers.
- the 76.60 percent who have no backup plan in case of early retirement.
- the 36.65 percent who had nothing they could think of that they had always wanted to in retirement.
- the 76.19 percent who didn't have their significant other participate in the retirement plan.

Not surprisingly, those I interviewed when writing this book all wish they had started not only planning earlier but also saving earlier, especially those who had to retire because of injury,

PTSD, or other reasons. Perhaps the most important part of planning—certainly the part having the most impact on whether or not you will be able to lead the lifestyle you would like—is dealing with finances. Remember, if you're not Medicare age, you will need to find affordable health insurance. You will still have cars that need upkeep, maintenance, and insurance. You will have cost-of-living increases to deal with along with rent or mortgage payments and home insurance. You might have moving expenses depending on where you want to settle.

Perhaps the most important part of planning—certainly the part having the most impact on whether or not you will be able to lead the lifestyle you would like—is dealing with finances.

And, yes, you will need to contend with taxes, which vary greatly from state to state. You won't be getting overtime pay to cover these costs, so, unless you plan to work, you will be living on a fixed income. It is suggested that six months to a year out, you start living off just your base pay to get an idea of what that looks and feels like. If you aren't able to comfortably pay your bills and still have money left over for fun, you will still have time to make the necessary adjustments.

To provide input on how to financially prepare for retirement, I spoke with Stephen Hall, a tax expert at Robert Hall & Associates who has long worked with first responders. He says, "Our founder Bob Hall was a volunteer EMT passionate about the work first responders do and wanted to contribute as much as he could." Stephen's experience with so many first responders has taught him that "Most are pretty cavalier. They assume the city or state pension will cover them when they retire and that overtime pay will always be available when they want the money. Unfortunately, that's not always the case."

I asked for three rules he thought were most important in enabling first responders to eventually retire with fewer tax issues or financial challenges. These are Stephen's choices.

1. Do not rely on overtime pay to buy your boat or cars.

2. Do not file "Exempt" and assume you will be okay on your taxes at the end of the year.

3. Read *Fully Involved* to prevent a divorce. Divorce is one of the most devastating actions in any person's life.

Taxes: Breaks and Takes

As I noted in the last chapter, when you're thinking of relocating, you have to look closely at what different states offer because the fifty components that make up the United States are far from united on taxation.

Stephen Hall has a list of tax-friendly states to recommend, based on what they offer and specifically what his first responder clients are seeking, noting, "Most families are retiring to lower their cost of living and be close to their family and healthcare centers." He says the states are "Tax-friendly states for retirees that have no state income tax, no taxes or a significant tax deduction on retirement income plus friendly sales, property, and estate or inheritance taxes." Based on these points, those states are Alaska, Florida, Georgia, Mississippi, Nevada, South Dakota, and Wyoming.

And, yes, there are states you may wish to avoid. Stephen says those are the ones that offer no retirement income tax benefits and don't have especially friendly sales, property, or estate and inheritance tax rates. The most recent numbers for 2021 are:

- California: Income tax rates range from just 1 percent to a whopping 12.5 percent. Sales tax is 7.255 percent to 10.755 percent.
- Connecticut: Income tax rates range from 3 percent to 6.99 percent. Sales tax is 6.35 percent.
- Maine: Income tax rates range from 5.8 percent to 7.15 percent. Sales tax is 5.5 percent.
- Minnesota: Income tax rates range from 5.35 percent to 9.85 percent. Sales tax is 6.875 percent.
- Nebraska: Income tax rates range 2.46 to 6.64% [2020]. Sales tax is 5.5.
- Rhode Island: Income tax rates range from 3.75 percent to 5.99 percent. Sales tax is 7 percent.
- Vermont: Income tax rates range from 3.35 percent to 8.75 percent. Sales tax is 6 percent.

Also, seventeen states allow counties and cities to impose separate taxes, which can add up to another 3.2 percent to your tax payments. As for property taxes, these range from a low of 0.4 percent in Alabama to a high of 2.42 percent in New Jersey.

That doesn't mean you should avoid looking into any of these states if that's where you long to go, but you should look closely at how much more of your retirement income living in any of them would cost you. Don't forget the cost of real estate in general. For instance, Hawaii offers some tax breaks, but real estate is priced so high, you might never be able to find what you have in mind for what you can afford. Stephen advises finding more information on the tax-friendly and tax-unfriendly states at https://smartasset.com/retirement/retirement-taxes.

Obviously, buying a home, whether you're selling one or wanting to move from a rental, is a major investment, never to be taken lightly—and certainly not in retirement, because you will probably move at some point and could very well move more than once. In a cnbc.com article from September 8, 2020 (https://

www.cnbc.com/2020/09/08/escape-winter-save-money-plan-fo
r-aging-why-people-move-in-retirement.html), Cyndi Hutchins,
Director of Gerontology at Bank of America Merrill Lynch in Bel
Air, Maryland, stated "Sixty-four percent of retirees say that they
are likely to move at least once during retirement." The reason?
The same reason Jeff and I bought a single-story home in Las
Vegas: the home you buy when you first retire and are younger
and more active might not meet your needs when you're older.
You'll certainly save money, not to mention your sanity, if you
don't need to move twice post-retirement.

"Sixty-four percent of retirees say that they are likely
to move at least once during retirement."

Another consideration raised in that same article is whether
to pay off your mortgage if you don't plan on moving. It might
seem wise to do so, but you need to consider the mortgage rates,
follow the market rates, and avoid rushing into things. If mortgage rates are low, you might want to pay yours off and have one
less thing to deal with every month. If they're high and you hang
in hoping they'll go down or even if they're low and you hope
they'll go even lower, you could end up losing some money you
might have gained income on elsewhere. Regardless, unless you
decide to pay off the balance right away when you retire or are
still working, you should keep an eye on those rates.

The best way to calculate is to check online, as the information is readily available and changes every year. When you do
your calculations, keep in mind that the higher the real estate
prices in any given area, the higher your property taxes will be
and that you may also be subject to local sales taxes. It might
sound like an overwhelming task figuring everything out, but a
tax or financial advisor can help you.

Know Who You Are and What You Want

Why might you want to meet with a professional advisor who can help you plan your retirement future? For one, that future is going to be very different financially from your past. Even if you have hefty savings in addition to your pension, things will change and if you have a spouse, their income will also be included in your tax obligations. Yes, you should listen to retired first responders about their experiences and why they chose to do things a certain way, but as Stephen says, "Every family is different and has different goals and family dynamics." And *when* a first responder retires it isn't the same for everyone. "Those that retire early due to a disability receive a nontaxable pension on a portion or all of their retirement. Those that are lucky to be injury-free when they retire will be taxed on 100 percent of their pension," he explains. You can't always apply someone else's situation to your own. But you should certainly listen to it and give thought to how their experiences might apply to you—and discuss that with your professional advisor.

Though Wesley ended up happily living in the house he built on his parcel of land in Utah, he admits that, financially, he could have done better, saying, "If I could have changed anything, it would have been to pay closer attention to a financial advisor I used to listen to on the radio. He was anti-debt, and he'd say not to buy a new car every year and not to refinance your house so you can use the money to pay something else. Ultimately, I ended up getting lucky in the long term because the house we'd bought and lived in, in Southern California, jumped up in value dramatically from when we'd bought it." What he did that was lucky but could have been disastrous was to refinance that house and buy one not far away to use as a rental.

"And that house was always a loser for us," he admits. "I was spending more on it each month than my renter was paying me, which wasn't ideal! But what ended up happening was that when it was time to pull the trigger and retire and move, those two houses became critical for us. I used the primary house as a source of equity by selling it, then I used some of that money to purchase the Utah property. I then used more of that money to get the renters out of the other California house and completely rehab it. Then we lived in it for our last two years before selling so I could get out from under capital gains taxes when we sold.

"Once we sold, we moved in temporarily with my daughter, then we left California free and clear. While it worked out beautifully, I can't say it was any part of a grandmaster plan that had been ten to fifteen years in the making. We were just living our lives—and then at the eleventh hour, I looked around and thought, *Okay, I could move these chess pieces around like this, and if everything falls into place, we'll be fine.* So, I was lucky that everything fell into place. I consider it luck because while we had a solid three-to-four-year plan, it should have been ten or even twenty years. Working with it in segments over time would have been smarter than basically cramming for finals. It worked out for us, but if I could go back and change it, I would."

The combination of an acceptable degree of pre-planning and getting lucky in the housing market helped Jeff and me as it did Wesley. Jeff knew he wanted to work and that he wanted something using the skills he had learned as a firefighter and battalion chief. Even though he wasn't excited about working for a utility, his work would have been fire-related. And we had contacts in both fire and law enforcement in Las Vegas (plus our daughter working in youth corrections). Rather than work in utilities, Jeff got the UNLV position as an Emergency Management Coordinator, and he enjoys being able to use his operations experience in dealing with large scale disaster management. I could work anywhere, but my contacts proved invaluable, and I now work with Henderson Fire and Police, Las Vegas Metro Police, and Clark County Fire as well as continuing to work with the federal and state agencies for crisis and debriefs.

Equally important, our decision of where to move practically made itself without our help, due to having a daughter and son-in-law here and a son who decided Las Vegas is where he wanted to live. Since my father also lives here and Jeff and I knew the area quite well, it was a shoo-in, especially given the tax situation. And, while the housing prices had started skyrocketing in the Las Vegas-Henderson area before our moving, they had also skyrocketed in Southern California, so we could get what we wanted without taking on a lot of debt.

But real estate is fickle, and you should be sure buying is the right option for you rather than perhaps renting for a year to wait out the market. And, because it *is* a gamble, while perhaps not as much of one as going to the track or shooting craps, it's always wise to get your advisor's opinion.

A worthwhile and life-impacting goal to achieve before retirement is changing your banking habits if you're used to living large. Paying off debt and socking away more savings will improve your life in retirement. If you have investments now, you will want to go over these with your advisor or broker as well, since banking on long-shot stocks or investment instruments like bonds with many years to reach maturity might not be your best option unless you are already knowledgeable about the markets and want to put aside a modest amount of mad money to try your hand at day-trading or picking emerging markets.

You aren't going to become another person, nor should you. You never give up your first responder identity. Even if you get a great job or hobby far removed from your previous life, you were a first responder for a long time, and that experience has formed you. Why go cold turkey? You can join or even create a support group for retired police, fire, corrections, EMT, or dispatch employees—a group that has had many identical or similar experiences and where others will always grasp what any member is talking about when discussing problems and challenges.

And, in terms of problems and challenges, I can't stress

enough the importance of getting any unresolved relationship problems dealt with before retiring. If you've read *Fully Involved*, you are aware of how important talking things through is in any relationship. When two people who haven't been used to being around each other constantly in years, if ever, any of the niggling issues either swept under the carpet will be there waiting to be set free. And I'm not talking about just disagreements, resentments you've been carrying, or things that annoy each other—I'm also talking about major things locked so deep into the mind's innermost closets you might not even be aware of them except when you wake in the middle in the night having fallen out of love, feeling the two of you have nothing in common anymore, or just feeling you're disconnected as a couple. You don't want any of that boiling over into your retirement. Talk things through calmly and without finger-pointing, see a counselor together, do whatever it takes to decide what can be done long before you're hanging up your badge or departmental ID.

In that first book, I discussed how to have rational discussions about major issues without blaming each other, without just washing your hands of a relationship that might be salvageable. I advised, and advise, all first responder couples to attend to their relationships regularly as part of their pre-retirement plan. Keep in mind that you *want* someone to retire with, and if that someone can be the person you've been with for ten or fifteen years or the major part of your life, so much better. Divorce or the breakup of any long-term life partnership for anyone with retirement around the corner is painful and difficult but sometimes the only solution. And, no matter when you do it, if you do it close to or after retiring, it will affect everything on your retirement agenda: your finances, where to live, your friendships. You will have to create a new version of your future and new plans for it.

So, clear the air and tell any truths you have been holding back. I have done a lot of couples counseling, and I know that relationships can not only be saved but can be strengthened in the process of talking things through. I know how much honesty and openness have kept Jeff's and my marriage loving and exciting. As two strong-willed, competitive individuals, it wasn't easy. Yet, as I tell couples who come to me for counseling, "The sign of a healthy relationship isn't that you don't fight. It's how you fight and how you resolve issues." The great beginning of our new life might not have been possible if we hadn't committed to hashing things out, gone into couples therapy ourselves, talking things through, working on our problems together, and giving each other space. These aren't just practical details—they're part of the stuff that matters most in life.

Points to Think About:

1. Your new life will require changes regardless of what you do or when you do it, but deciding where to live is a must, and much of that decision revolves around financial planning. It's never too soon to start meeting with your financial planner or researching on your own the possibility of moving out of state for tax breaks—especially if you aren't planning on a second career. You need to decide on what you want, what you can easily afford, and what you might be willing to give to make your retirement easier and more enjoyable.

2. As you get closer to retirement, it's more important than ever to increase your knowledge about benefits you might be entitled to, any frivolous spending habits you might need to choose between if you want to have the retirement you envision, and what things matter to you. What can't you imagine life without? What would be an ideal day in your new life? Ideal week? Fantastic year? No one else is going to make it happen for you. An advisor can help you find your way on the path, but you and your significant other will be setting the rules.

3. Your significant other is the person of prime importance in your life, so it's imperative to have total openness and share what each of you wants out of the rest of your lives together. Seek couples counseling if there are serious issues in your relationship. Seek agreement if there are minor questions to be resolved. Retiring without marital discord is one of the "must-haves" for a nice, smooth slide into that future.

The New You

And here we are. We've reached the end of the book but just the beginning of your planning for your new life. Meanwhile, Jeff and I will reach the end of Year One of our new life June 1, 2022. We hit the ground running: I opened my office July 1, 2021, and Jeff started his new job October 15. While we have faced, and will undoubtedly face more, challenges and adjustments, we are pretty relaxed along with being content. You will be, too, if you prepare and do as much as you can to get the details down ahead of time.

We're lucky. We never doubted our decision on where to move, a decision based on factors that included being close to our kids, sticking to a good state in terms of costs and taxes, avoiding drastic changes of weather, and settling in an area that offered good work prospects for us both, Jeff as a full-timer and me as a consulting clinician. As I said earlier, it still takes getting used to for any first responder family, not only because it's all new but because—unlike many retirees—Jeff was leaving a job that was more than just a job, that was a way of life. When you retire as a first responder, you are leaving a family behind, your work family. You're also leaving behind a regimented way of life and defined purpose. The last strikes most people at first as a fabulous gift, a blessing of sorts. But life is complex, and so is retiring as a first responder. Your schedule is no longer there for you, rigid and precise. You have to create your new schedule on your own and get used to having some flexibility.

If you start a new career, you will also need to adjust to that, especially if you're joining the "civilian" workforce. Even Jeff, who's a master of rolling with the punches, finds some of it puzzling and challenging. He still isn't quite sure how to handle lunch. When he asked his coworkers what they did for lunch, the answer was "You can do whatever you want. We pretty much do our own thing and eat when we're hungry." After having had lunch prepared for him and eating with his crews for thirty-four years, lunch by himself was weird and uncomfortable. He's gotten used to it, but it's taken time.

If you take a regular job with weekends and holidays off, you might have no idea what that means. Jeff didn't have a clue about how to plan accordingly, and on Veterans Day, he was at loose ends. It fell on a Thursday so that was a holiday, but it hadn't occurred to Jeff that his coworkers at the university would take off Friday as well to have a four-day weekend. It was a bit freaky for him to find himself all alone at the office when he showed up Friday morning.

And, as I said, his Monday-to-Friday schedule has been a challenge to us both. We took so much for granted! Both of us were used to being able to get a lot of things done during the week when nothing was as busy. Now Jeff has to figure out how to get some things done as a five-day-a-week-with-weekends-off employee—scheduling regular workouts when the gym isn't at top capacity, for example, or dealing with car maintenance issues. I've been impacted as well. Even though I can get more done because I'm not any organization's full-time employee, Jeff's schedule means we can't have date nights during the week when there aren't so many people around (and when more bargains on entertainment can be found). It also means that I have to try to do more of my own things during the week when I'm working so we can have more quality time together on Saturdays and Sundays. Then the weekend comes and we often feel like we're having to rush around to cram everything in. That makes me sad at times, but I know we'll adjust to connecting on the weekends like everyone else. We *are* everyone else now.

I am thankful every day that Jeff and I planned for his retirement, even if it would have been even better had we planned farther in advance. But any and all preparation pays off. Planning also helps reduce some of the fears and anxiety that come with retirement looming ahead. Those worries are only natural; after all, retiring from active duty as a first responder is one of the biggest steps in anyone's career. But having narrowed your preferences of whether or not to relocate, where to go, what type of property to look for, and what you require as necessities versus what you'd like as bonuses will make starting your new life easier.

Pre-retirement provides a welcome chance to clear out the clutter in your house and your head. Dealing with relationship, financial, and wish-list issues is the most important. Too many loose ends too close to calling it quits will make retirement more confusing and stressful. You needn't have everything written in stone, but it's going to help incredibly if you have a folder of things you can mark as resolved and move on to enjoying your new life.

As far as things go, get rid of what you don't need or love. Possessions, while we need and cherish many of them, can also weigh us down, make a new home seem too small or too cluttered, fill our lives with the past rather than the future. There is a genuine feeling of freedom when you cast off things you've held onto too long, especially things like that weight set you haven't touched in thirty years or the collection of jars and tins you've been hoarding because you were certain you would find a use for all of them one day. Enough. Let someone else enjoy your hand-me-downs: they will be new and interesting to them.

Your Final "Honey Do" Lists

Here's a general recap of what you can and should start doing as soon as you close this book. First of all, you need to pre-plan your retirement on three levels. Why? Because you don't know what the future holds. You need to be prepared to retire as a lifer, which might be far into the future if you're young, and even as a lifer, you might decide to leave early for a new career. It happens. If you're young and planning to retire as a lifer, good for you. You have plenty of time to do what most retired first responders tell me they wish they had done and save more money. You also need to be ready in case you suffer an injury or illness that forces you to retire. The people you heard from in these pages who had to retire hadn't planned on getting hurt or sick, and it took its toll on them. The same holds for retiring early because of PTSD. *It can never happen to me* is easy to think until it does. It's nothing to be shy about or ashamed of—you have one of the most stressful and often trauma-inducing jobs in the world—and you need to consider the possibility in your planning.

If you're close to retirement age and haven't thought about planning anything more than sleeping late and going fishing or on beach vacations, it's time to start thinking fast. You are going to be building a whole new life—without all the time to do it in that you spent building your current one. Whether you will retire as an empty nester, a family with kids still at home, or a single or divorced person with no one to share your days and nights, you need to have a plan. You need to know ahead of leaving the job what you want next. Is it a second career? A move to a new location and/or a different home? A plan for seeing the USA or the world with travel as your main objective? You have a multitude of choices, and if you have a significant other, they probably have some ideas as well.

Even though you're still on the job, you need to be aware that your Work Brain is going to keep functioning after you leave and that it will shove Home Brain out of the way. Becoming a regular civilian takes time, and this abrupt change in your life, even if you know it was coming, will affect you and those close to you. You need to know what to expect and be prepared for Work Brain trying to dictate your emotions and actions. You can become, frankly, impossible by being home all the time, with a spouse 24/7, trying to be more active in raising your kids to make up for not having been there enough when working, and wanting to be the boss all day every day.

Your brain unpacking when you retire is normal, but it means some of your old calls will come back to haunt you, causing anxiety, nightmares, an aversion to going to certain places, and even feeling traumatized. You can help through a clinician and through scheduling EMDR sessions to relive and desensitize any traumatic calls so you're prepared to deal with them if they pop up in your head again.

Perhaps most of all, you need to actively start building your new life before you need it. That means getting a head start on hobbies and finding things you like to do. Keep lists of things that spark your interest or that you used to love until life got in the way. You can't sleep late forever, and that path leads to depression. You're used to having a schedule, and you will need one when you retire.

When to do what? Long-term considerations such as moving to a new state can start at any time, the sooner the better if you need to narrow down choices. If you're pretty sure you will want to live in a smaller place when you retire, you can start clearing out anytime starting tomorrow. It's always good to continually get rid of things you're saving for no good reason at all other than "Hmm, this might come in handy one day."

Other things should go on your Five- and One-Year Lists, and you should start doing those as soon as you're that far from your planned retirement. Here's a quick hit list for you.

FIVE-YEAR PLAN

- Make an appointment with PERS or whatever retirement organization will be handling your pension.
  - › Check what your payout will be.
  - › Find out what it will cost to include your spouse as a beneficiary and survivor (these are two separate categories in Retirement Land).
- Start looking at health insurance costs and gathering information on the best options on a state-by-state basis if you have an idea where you will be living.
- Plot out your deferred compensation goals.
- Check out the opportunity for promotion and how it will affect your retirement.
  - › Example: Will your payout be based on your single highest year or the average of three years?
- If you plan to move out of state, start visiting the area during vacation times and get to know the lay of the land.
  - › Research the rules on establishing residency in that state before retiring.
- Speak with your financial planner about what you can do to be better prepared.
  - › Ask about selling your home, paying it off, and the tax benefits (or drawbacks) for the state you wish to live in.
- Planning to start a new career or get a job? Start looking in the area you might be interested in. You needn't zero in on a specific job so early, but you will want to see what possibilities exist. Along with your first responder network, there are many websites that can help, as long as you know what you want to do.
- Start paying down debt and stop incurring any new debt.

ONE-YEAR PLAN

- Make another appointment with PERS or whatever retirement organization will be handling your pension.
  - › Get an updated figure on what your payout will be.
  - › Find out what it will now cost to include your spouse as a beneficiary and survivor (these are two separate categories in Retirement Land).
- Make an appointment with a clinician to process any old calls lurking around in your brain.
- Strengthen your relationship with your significant other and commit to talking through and resolving any issues immediately.
- Get a good grasp of your leave-hours accruals and cash-out options.
  - › Talk with a financial planner to decide what is the best option for you.
- Start applying for jobs that interest you.
  - › As much as you can from wherever you are, strive to build a network with people doing what you'd like to do who might recommend you or provide good leads.
- If you will be moving, start looking at homes or property.
  - › Purge! This is the right time to start cleaning out your closet, garage, basement, and attic. Sell what you can, then donate what you don't need and get the tax write-off.
  - › Even if you plan to stay in the same area, if you'll be downsizing, start looking. And keep an eye on the market and the interest rates. (This applies to selling your current home as well if you plan on doing so.)
- Start something new or rediscover something old.
  - › Explore new hobbies or classes that interest you.

- > Look for any groups or clubs where you live or will be living that are geared toward your interests (such as ski clubs, running groups, hiking associations) as well as charities that need local volunteers.
- Start attempting to live off base pay to know how tight your budget is.
  - > Either decrease your overtime or put that extra income into a savings account.
  - > If you still have debt, use that extra money to finish paying it off.

You Can Do It

Retirement planning covers many areas and eventualities, but don't be daunted. Remember, parts of it—learning about lifestyle options and new places, planning hobbies and travel, choosing and fixing up a new home—are entertaining and fun. And while too many first responders have regrets after retirement, most of those regrets are about NOT planning and never about the planning they did manage to achieve. You can do it as long as you remember the two biggest points: Be Prepared and Stay Open to New Experiences. You have worked all your life for this. You deserve to enjoy it.

When the calls stop coming, you might feel alone and at loose ends at first. Your life may seem to have lost much of its meaning, but its meaning is who you are now that you have retired and not what you were when you were working. It's time for a second fulfilling career, an interesting part-time job, rewarding volunteer work, more time for sports and hobbies, discovering new and exciting things to do and places to go.

Sure, it's challenging, but let me leave with these words: Jeff and I did it, and challenges and all, we're loving it. Start planning now, and you will, too!

Bryan
2025

Made in United States
Troutdale, OR
11/01/2024

24336379R00080